To Nancy & Grady,

Best wishes to
devoted Redskins fans.
Enjoy the memories!

Stadium Stories:
# Washington Redskins

Stadium Stories™ Series

Stadium Stories:

# Washington Redskins

John Keim

INSIDERS' GUIDE®

GUILFORD, CONNECTICUT
AN IMPRINT OF THE GLOBE PEQUOT PRESS

**INSIDERS' GUIDE**®

Text design: Casey Shain
Cover photos: *front cover:* defense (Tim Sharp/AP); *back cover:* top, the Hogs (AP); bottom, Joe Gibbs with the Lombardi trophy (Doug Mills/AP)

Library of Congress Cataloging-in-Publication Data

Keim, John.
    Stadium stories : Washington Redskins / John Keim.— 1st ed.
        p. cm. — (Stadium stories series)
    ISBN 0-7627-3780-8
        1. Washington Redskins (Football team)—History. I. Title. II. Series.

GV956.W3K45 2005
796.332'64'09753—dc22                                              2005047455


Manufactured in the United States of America
First Edition/First Printing

To my father and brothers, Bobby, Neil, and Chris, with whom I miss sharing football Sundays. And to my three sons, Matthew, Christopher, and Sean, with whom I hope to share many such days. Finally, to the Redskins fans, for their extreme loyalty and passion.

# Contents

# Acknowledgments

**It's impossible to tackle** a project like this without getting plenty of help. My name is on the cover, but without dozens of other people, there would be no book.

Without the fans' passion, there'd be no interest. Without the players' accomplishments, there would be few stories worth retelling. And without the cooperation of many, many people, this book would never have been written.

Let's start with the players, coaches, and other staff, nearly three dozen of whom I interviewed for this project. I'd also talked with numerous other players in the past and have used their words in this book as well. There are too many names to mention, but my gratitude for their time and cooperation is endless.

And the Redskins public relations staff, Pat Wixted and Will Norman in particular, were gracious in allowing me access to clip files.

Longtime beat reporter Jim Ducibella of the *Virginian Pilot* is a terrific friend, and without him I wouldn't have written this book. I'm glad he turned me on to this project. His confidence in me and his encouragement mean the world.

I'd also like to thank Dan Rubin, sports editor for the *Washington Examiner*, and Dave Jones, publisher of *Warpath*, for their continued support.

The Globe Pequot Press has been terrific to work with, from executive editor Mary Norris to consulting editor Mike Urban. I love writing books, but it's even better when working with quality people.

But nothing could be done without my family, particularly my ultrapatient and highly understanding wife, Kerry. Simply put, she's the best. My boys, Matthew, Christopher, and Sean, always provide me with motivation, even when they don't know it. And my mother has always been very supportive of my work. Without their support, these projects would not be worth doing.

Thanks to all of you.

# In the Beginning

The pilot alerted the Redskins over the intercom to a situation at the airport. Washington had energized the area with a 20–16 win at Dallas, its third straight win. And fans, sensing something big for the first time in eons, couldn't wait to celebrate. It didn't matter that eleven games remained in the 1971 season. So they flocked to Dulles Airport, and the pilot relayed the scene to the Redskins as they prepared to land. "You can see cars for miles down Dulles Access Road," he told the team. "They're backed up trying to get to the airport!" But it didn't end there.

"We land at the freight terminal and walk off the plane and they have us wait," recalled Bubba Tyer, then in his first season as a trainer. "The pilot said, 'There's a crowd out there!' Then they opened the doors outside the terminal and there's 8,000 people out there screaming."

After decades of frustration, the Redskins had finally appeared on the verge of being special—just as they were when they first came to Washington in 1937, setting a tone that made the Redskins more than just another NFL team. The reason there's so much passion surrounding the franchise now is because of the success they had in the beginning. Look at the attendance figures from the early 1960s and on. After years of mediocre or bad football—no playoff appearances since 1945— the Redskins, with no end to the losing in sight, started selling out games, largely due to the addition of offensive standouts such as Sonny Jurgensen, Bobby Mitchell, and Charley Taylor. They haven't stopped yet.

Yes, they won three Super Bowls from 1982 to 1992, helping fuel the fans' passion for all things Redskins—500,000 turned out for a parade following their first Super Bowl title. But since winning their last Super Bowl after the 1991 season, the Redskins made only one playoff appearance between 1992 and 2004. Yet during that time they moved into the NFL's largest stadium, with a seating capacity of 91,665. "The fans feel they're a part of the team," said former quarterback Mark Rypien. "It's the total community."

That support was there in the beginning, too. In the Redskins' first season in Washington, more than 10,000 fans ventured to New York to watch them win the season finale, clinching a division title. Another 5,000 greeted the team at Union Station upon its return to Washington. A week later, another 3,000 headed for the championship at Chicago, making up one-fifth of the crowd on a frigid day.

That early success stemmed from the combined efforts of an owner with a showbiz mentality, a future Hall of Famer at quarterback, and a future Hall of Fame coach. Together they made the Redskins a formidable squad, one that would win two NFL titles in its first six seasons in Washington—and lose two other times.

Good thing for Washington that Boston didn't want the Redskins. In 1932, Washington, D.C., laundry shop owner George Preston Marshall and three other investors bought the new Boston Braves. A year later, playing in Fenway Park, Marshall renamed them the Redskins (and hired an Indian coach named Lone Star Dietz).

They weren't profitable, losing $46,000 the first season and causing Marshall's three other investors to drop out. Marshall had a hard time selling his team to the public. Newspapers rarely wrote about them. Fans rarely attended. In 1936 the Redskins reached the NFL championship, losing to Green Bay. However, they drew fewer than 14,000 fans to each of the seven home games.

Enter Washington. Marshall moved the team to the nation's capital for the 1937 season and was instantly welcomed. In seven games that final season in Boston, the Redskins drew 57,363 fans. In six games that first season in Washington, they drew 120,022 fans.

In addition to support, they had something else in Washington they didn't have in Boston: Sammy Baugh. The rookie joined three other future Hall of Famers on the roster. One of them was star running back Cliff Battles. Marshall first noticed Battles when he played a game for West Virginia Wesleyan against Georgetown. A year earlier, Battles had scored on touchdown runs of 90, 96, and 98 yards. Marshall wanted him badly. So he sent a group to West Virginia, telling them not to return until Battles was signed. And for his part, Battles made Marshall look smart, rushing for 3,622 yards between 1932 and 1937, a figure no other back had approached.

But Washington didn't have much of a chance to appreciate Battles. After the 1937 season, Battles wanted a raise from his salary of $2,800. Marshall balked, having just awarded Baugh a three-year, $10,000 deal. So Battles quit professional football to become an assistant coach at Columbia University—for $4,000 per season.

Another player from that 1936 draft also figured prominently in Washington's early success. Receiver Wayne Millner wasn't selected until the eighth round. But second-year coach Ray Flaherty knew all about Millner. In college, Millner gained a national reputation when he helped Notre Dame rally for an 18–13 win at Ohio State in the "Game of the Century." Millner's 19-yard touchdown catch with fewer than thirty seconds remaining punctuated the comeback and helped him become a consensus All-American.

That made Flaherty salivate at the thought of having Millner. Flaherty said he would resign "if we don't win the championship with that big Yankee playing end." He didn't have to worry about fulfilling that promise, as the Redskins won a title the following season.

Millner soon established himself as one of football's top players, starring at end on offense and defense. He would finish with

*Quarterback Sammy Baugh, center, celebrates with teammates Cliff Battles, left, and Wayne Millner after winning the National Football League Championship Game in 1937. AP*

numbers that look puny by today's standards, but they were good enough to land him in the Hall of Fame. Millner caught 124 passes for 1,578 yards and 12 touchdowns. Of course, those numbers would have been better had World War II not interrupted his career. Millner, who played one more season after the war, saved his best for crucial situations, earning the label as a "money player."

The third future Hall of Famer on Washington's roster was captain and two-way tackle, Turk Edwards. Considered big for his era at 260 pounds, Edwards dominated. Edwards was an original Boston Brave, signing in 1932. He earned All-Pro honors in 1932, 1933, 1936, and 1937. In 1934 and 1938 he was named second-team All-Pro. But a bad knee slowed him and, in 1940, ended his career, in fluke fashion. After representing the Redskins for the coin toss before a game versus the New York Giants, Edwards headed toward the bench. His career would end before he got there. His knee, bothered by sustained ligament damage, buckled. He would play only one more game for Washington.

The Redskins enjoyed success under Flaherty, who took over in 1936. Marshall didn't have much luck with coaches before Flaherty, or after him for that matter. From 1936 to 1942, the Redskins went 54–21–3 and won two championships. They went 20–8–2 with two World Championship losses in the first three years after Flaherty, under two different coaches. But of Washington's next nine coaches, only one finished with a winning record in his Redskins career—Dick Todd went 5–4 in 1951, his only season as coach.

But Flaherty was different. He was an innovator and he was smart, qualities that were evident a few years before he became the Redskins coach. In the 1934 NFL title game, the field at the Polo Grounds was frozen. Flaherty, then a Giants player, figured it would be better to wear basketball shoes rather than cleats. The move was made and New York upset heavily favored Chicago, 30–13.

Marshall, who had hired and fired three other coaches since 1932, hired Flaherty and reaped immediate rewards. In the season before Flaherty arrived, Washington finished 2–8–1. In Flaherty's first season, and with eleven rookies, the Redskins went 7–5 and reached the Eastern Division title game.

Expectations increased in 1937, thanks to the addition of Baugh. His addition helped generate the hype Marshall needed—and wanted—to sell tickets in a new city. Marshall had spread the word that this season would be special, not just because it was the first in Washington (though that certainly helped draw more than 1,000 fans to the first workout). Baugh enabled them to surpass the hype, thanks to his second-year coach's wisdom. Though Baugh was not considered a quarterback—Riley Smith played that position—he was in charge of passing from the Single Wing attack.

Flaherty started devising plays to make sure defenses couldn't hurt his prized player, leading to his first innovation—the screen pass. Though it would be tweaked over time to fit the T-formation, Flaherty's version fit the Single Wing and Double Wing sets, with the line sliding right or left and Baugh receiving the snap at halfback. He introduced the screen in 1937, stunning the Chicago Bears in the season finale. On the first play of the game, Baugh passed to Battles behind the line of scrimmage and he raced 55 yards. It was the first of many big plays in a 28–21 victory. Millner, crafting his reputation, caught two touchdown passes from Baugh.

In 1942 Flaherty developed the two-platoon system, using one set of players for the ground game and another one for the passing game. Once again, it worked as the Redskins rolled to their second title. "He had a brilliant mind," tackle Jim Barber once told the *Washington Post*. "He could handle players. He knew when to kick you in the fanny and pat you on the back. Everyone respected him. Sammy had eight coaches with the Redskins, but Ray was the best by far."

It wasn't just his ability to tinker with new plays or formations, it was his demanding ways that helped produce winners. Flaherty, nicknamed Red, was himself a tough two-way end for the Giants from 1928 to 1929 and from 1931 to 1935. He carried those gruff ways with him into coaching. Once, before a matchup with Chicago, Flaherty told reporters, "If the Bears want to get tough in the clinches, we'll get tough, too. If there's some rough stuff, we're going to be in on it."

Reporters were allowed in the locker room before games, providing an opportunity to hear Flaherty's speeches. He liked to excite his players, as he did before the Redskins' first game in Washington. "We're playing in a new town, and you guys have got to make good for the fans," he told them. "We're paying you for only sixty minutes of football a week, and I want sixty good minutes."

He also wanted Baugh protected, reminding the players that some of them had complained about the lack of a passer for three years. They had one now, and they needed him healthy. "You know damn well those Giants will be out to cut Sammy down the first chance they get and try to get him out of there," he told them. "You know damn well what I want you to do. Don't let 'em get to Sammy, understand?"

The Redskins then went out and beat New York, 13–3, in front of 25,000 spectators. But it wasn't because of Baugh. Smith scored

Coach Ray Flaherty, left, and owner George Preston Marshall congratulate each other after winning the 1937 NFL championship. AP

# Winning Ways

Ray Flaherty has the best winning percentage among all-time Redskins coaches. In seven seasons from 1936 to 1942, Flaherty posted a 54-21-3 record for a .712 percentage. But Joe Gibbs has the best postseason mark with a 16-5 record for a percentage of .762.

all the points, booting two 18-yard field goals and clinching the win with a 60-yard interception return for a touchdown.

Helped by Flaherty's guidance, a love affair began. He proved to be the one coach who could buck Marshall's theatrical ways. The Redskins owner liked to stand on the sidelines and berate the officials or offer suggestions to coaches. He tried this with Flaherty once, telling him to use a certain player. Flaherty supposedly responded, "If you want me to coach, get back up in the seats. If you want to coach, take over right now and I'll go back home." Marshall retreated to the owner's box and never bothered Flaherty again.

Not that he could complain about much as the Redskins became one of the NFL's best teams. But after the 1942 championship win over Chicago, Flaherty was headed for the navy. He would serve until 1945. Even though the Redskins had an opening, Marshall, who liked to be in control and could not dominate Flaherty, looked elsewhere for a coach.

However, before Flaherty left—and for a couple seasons afterward—the Redskins played in many big games, starting with the

1937 title game against Chicago. That game also started one of the league's best rivalries—one that easily matched the Redskins-Cowboys rivalry of the 1970s and 1980s—as the Bears and Redskins would play four times for the World Championship between 1937 and 1943. Both teams won twice—and they also split four regular-season meetings in that stretch. They detested one another, and the 1937 championship game provided the spark for that hatred—especially on Chicago's side, as Washington won 28–21 on frozen turf at Wrigley Field.

To reach the final, Washington had to win at New York. Marshall made sure the Redskins had enough support, bringing with them the 150-piece marching band and more than 10,000 fans. When they arrived in New York, Marshall led an impromptu parade down Seventh Avenue with the fans singing "Hail to the Redskins." They left in an even better mood after Washington's 49–14 victory. Battles provided much reason to cheer. During the game, Battles ran 75 yards to the 5, setting up his own rushing touchdown; he also ran for another touchdown and intercepted a pass, setting up a Smith score. This offensive explosion came against a team that had allowed only 60 points before this game.

Baugh and the Redskins offense were clicking. But they would be tested against Chicago. On this day Battles and Millner showed why they were considered among the best in the NFL, each playing a big role in the victory. First, Battles scored to make it 7–0. However, the Bears rallied for a 14–7 lead and, in the process, knocked Baugh from the game. Baugh hurt his knee near the end of the first half, keeping him out until early in the second half. Part of the problem was Baugh's defense. While playing safety, he too often had to tackle Bronko Nagurski. "No matter where I was, he'd come right at me," he once told writer

Roland Lazenby. "After the game I asked him why he kept coming after me. He said, 'I'll tell you why. I was supposed to run over you and get you out of the game.'"

It worked—for a while. When a limping Baugh reentered, he quickly fired a 55-yard touchdown pass to Millner, tying the score. Chicago scored once again, but Baugh answered with a 77-yard scoring toss to Millner. His third touchdown throw in ten minutes, a 35-yard pass to Ed Justice, finished the scoring.

An incident during this game only heightened the tension between the teams. Baugh tackled Chicago's Dick Plasman out of bounds on the Redskins sideline. A pile of players fell onto Plasman. When the officials pulled the players off him, they discovered Redskins trainer Roy Baker on top of Plasman. According to *Washington Daily News* reporter Robert Ruark, Baker was "trying to bite his initials into Plasman's ear."

Two years later, in their first rematch, the Bears won 31–7. Marshall stormed to the sidelines during this game, saying nothing to Flaherty but visibly upset. Bears coach George Halas tweaked Marshall even more after the game by telling reporters, "I'm awfully sorry my boys were a little rough."

The Bears would get their championship revenge in 1940. And it was ugly. After missing out on the postseason in 1938 and 1939, the Redskins returned to glory in 1940. They opened the season with seven straight wins. After losing to Brooklyn, Washington beat the Bears 7–3 in a preview of the championship. It was hardly a proper foreshadowing. In this game the Redskins held Chicago scoreless on six trips inside the 40 in the second half. Afterward, Marshall called the Bears quitters, predicting the Bears would have to win big or "they won't win at all."

No worry. The Bears won big. Real big.

"We had one of the best teams we ever had," Baugh told Lazenby. "That was just a game where we didn't hit a lick, and Mr. Marshall had given the Bears plenty of motivation." In a score that still stands as the most lopsided in professional football, Chicago beat host Washington 73–0 in front of 36,034 fans at Griffith Stadium. The only memorable moment for Washington came after the game. With the Redskins trailing 7–0, Charley Malone dropped a certain touchdown pass. When reporters asked Baugh if a catch would have changed the game, the quarterback said yes. "The score would have been 73–7."

The Redskins had to wait two years to exact their revenge. But they did. After going 6–5 in 1941, they recovered with a 10–1 record in 1942, losing only to the Giants in week two. But their nine-game winning streak paled compared to Chicago's eighteen-game winning streak entering the championship. The Bears, who had outscored their last five opponents 199–14, entered as massive favorites. This time the Bears provided pregame motivation as a report in Chicago said the Bears considered Baugh "the most overrated passer in football." Flaherty just happened to be in Chicago the day that story appeared.

Military duty was interrupting the sport as Halas, in uniform, watched from the Bears sideline. He had flown to D.C. from Oklahoma, where he was a lieutenant commander in the navy. Baugh put on a show for him and the 36,006 fans in attendance, leading this huge upset. He averaged more than 50 yards a punt, including an 85-yarder on a quick kick into the wind. That punt eventually provided Washington good field position after a Wilbur Moore interception. Baugh followed with a 39-yard touchdown pass to Moore for a 7–6 lead. Andy Farkas added a 1-yard touchdown run in the third quarter.

Then it was up to the defense, which came through twice to stop drives. Baugh intercepted a pass after Chicago had reached Washington's 15. With fewer than three minutes remaining in the game, the Bears drove to the Redskins' 2. But one apparent touchdown was nullified by a penalty and a fourth-down pass was incomplete, turning the ball over to the Redskins.

The fans celebrated in style, tearing down the goalposts. The team posed for a picture, recording this joyous occasion. But Flaherty had little time to celebrate: He was reporting to the navy in two days. His Redskins career had just ended.

But the Redskins didn't yet tumble into the bottom half of the league. Twice more they reached the NFL title game, but they lost both—in 1943 and 1945. Baugh missed most of the 1943 loss because of a concussion, suffered when he was kicked in the head trying to tackle Bears quarterback Sid Luckman. With Baugh out, the Redskins lost 41–21. As Baugh watched he cried out, "Why won't they let me play!" while teammates comforted him.

The 1945 title loss, at least, was to someone else. This time host Cleveland Rams sent them home disappointed on another frozen day. The temperature never rose above 6 degrees as the Redskins bundled up in parkas on the sidelines, where they also used hay to stay warm. Second-year coach Dudley DeGroot agreed to Rams coach Adam Walsh's request to not have his team wear sneakers and, in opting for sportsmanship, cost the Redskins the game.

Both teams struggled with the footing. But it was the goalposts that figured in the most crucial plays of the game. First, Baugh, passing from his own end zone, hit the crossbar, an automatic safety giving the Rams a 2–0 lead. Ironically, it was

Marshall who helped get the goal posts moved to the front of the end zone a few years earlier (he would also help get the safety rule changed in 1946). Later in the game, Cleveland's Bob Waterfield kicked an extra point that was partially blocked. But it hit the crossbar and bounced over, the difference in a 15–14 Rams victory.

Marshall, angered by DeGroot's agreement, soon fired his coach. But that wouldn't help change the Redskins fortunes. A golden era had ended. Another one wouldn't begin for twenty-five years.

# The Owners

From the beginning, to own the Redskins has been to own Washington. The owner of the Redskins has always hosted the elite of Washington society, turning its box into the place to be on Sundays. But Washington's owners also have been more than just hosts. They've been controversial, colorful, and powerful forces in the league. Some have even been champions, or at least helped build them. Clearly, one thing they haven't been is dull.

# George Preston Marshall

Redskins owner George Preston Marshall started a band, had a song crafted that lives to this day, and revolutionized the marketing of the NFL. When he found a player he wanted, he made sure to sign him with the Redskins, creating a blueprint for another Redskins owner sixty years later. He also interfered with his coaches—sometimes during games—and fired them often, creating a reputation for impatience—another blueprint.

As much as anything, however, George Preston Marshall is remembered for failing to integrate his roster until forced to do so in 1962. For years, *Washington Post* columnist Shirley Povich referred to the Redskins colors as "burgundy, gold, and Caucasian."

The Marshall story is a complex one. From the time he was a kid, Marshall showed a penchant for creativity. At nine, Marshall wanted to sell a common rabbit. Others sold similar rabbits for 40 cents. But he advertised it as a "Jacksonville Hare" and sold it for $1.25.

His family eventually turned to the laundry business, which Marshall inherited upon his father's death in 1918. Eventually, Marshall, who once owned a team in the American Basketball League and often followed baseball's Washington Senators on the road, bought an NFL franchise in Boston. Five years later, in 1937, he moved the Boston Redskins to his native Washington.

That's when the fun began for Marshall, not to mention Washington. His second wife, Corinne Griffith, whom he married in 1936, wrote the lyrics for "Hail to the Redskins." Marshall hired a band to play at games and was the first to put on halftime shows. The arrival of Santa Claus in December became one tradition. Would he come by parachute (once landing outside the stadium)? By helicopter? By motorcycle?

Marshall also was the first to create a vast radio network, turning the Redskins into the South's team. Their success, helped by the combination of quarterback Sammy Baugh and coach Ray Flaherty, made them easy to market. Marshall also had Cliff Battles, a star running back. Because Marshall wanted Battles so badly, he dispatched a Redskins contingent to the player's house in West Virginia. Battles chose Boston over Portsmouth and the New York Giants because of that ploy. But Baugh was the one Marshall marketed to the public, using him as a drawing card. "He told me the game needed to be opened up for the fans' entertainment," Baugh once said. "And that I should keep passing the ball, whether we were winning or losing. 'Don't pay any attention to the coach,' he said."

Marshall rarely did. Once, while the team was in Boston, he told coach Lone Star Dietz to kick off if they won the toss. When Marshall reached his seat, he saw the Redskins receiving. So he phoned down to the bench and shouted, "Dammit, I thought I told you to kick off." To which Dietz replied, "Where have you been George? We did kick off, and they ran it back for a touchdown."

Another time, Baugh overheard Marshall and coach John Whelchel arguing, with the owner saying numerous players were at wrong positions. Whelchel ignored the suggestions. But that only angered Marshall, who, at a later practice, stormed out of his car and yelled at Whelchel for not making the changes, causing Whelchel to leave. Marshall had Baugh, Dick Todd, and Wilbur Moore run practice. "And he had just hired Whelchel to be a disciplinarian!" Baugh later said.

But the other owners often listened to Marshall's suggestions. Within two years, he convinced them to move the goalposts to the goal line and then to split the league into two divisions, playing a championship game at the end of the season. He also forced a change in the rule regarding forward passes, allowing teams to throw from anywhere behind the line of scrimmage. Another Marshall idea: the Pro Bowl game. "The game was getting too dull," Marshall said.

He loved seeing his name in the papers. Before the 1940 NFL Championship Game, he called the Bears "quitters" and "front-runners." Chicago won 73–0. So after the game, Marshall stormed into the Redskins locker room and shouted, "They quit! Some of our players were yellow . . . There'll be plenty of new faces next year."

"A lot of boys hated that," Baugh said. "They hated what Mr. Marshall was putting out."

Others hated what Marshall stood for regarding civil rights, becoming the last to integrate his roster. Finally, in 1961, Secretary of the Interior Stewart Udall forced Marshall to integrate the roster by threatening to evict the Redskins from new D.C. Stadium, which was built on federal property. President Kennedy, promising an aggressive stance on civil rights, fully backed Udall. Marshall balked, wanting to know what law he had broken. He also said, "We'll start signing Negroes when the Harlem Globetrotters start signing whites."

After further pressure from an embarrassed league, Marshall agreed and, in December of 1961, he traded the first overall pick in the draft to Cleveland for star African-American running back Bobby Mitchell. Later that month, Washington drafted several black players, and eighth-round pick Ron Hatcher became the first to sign with the Redskins. They also traded for guard John Nisby, another African-American. "He never came across to me as a bigot," Mitchell said.

Still, when Marshall's career is discussed, it's hard to focus on one aspect. And he clearly turned the Redskins into the desired Washington social activity, even as the team stumbled through the 1950s and 1960s. Health reasons forced Marshall to cease day-to-day operations of the franchise in 1963, the same year he was voted into the Hall of Fame.

At his funeral in 1969, then-commissioner Pete Rozelle said, "His fertile imagination and vision brought vital improvements to the structure and presentation of the game. Pro football today does in many ways reflect his personality. It was his imagination, style, zest, dedication, openness, brashness, strength, and courage. We all are beneficiaries of what his dynamic personality helped shape over more than three decades."

## Jack Kent Cooke

The billionaire owner walked into an employee's office, demanding to know the results of his investigative work. Then he handed the employee, who was a member of football's Hall of Fame, his own list regarding the same issue. As Bobby Mitchell studied the list, seeing a bottom-line cost, he concluded one thing: He had more work to do. He called a few more people, whittled the price down, and turned in a new list, one that Jack Kent Cooke applauded. All this over the price of hot dogs for a team barbecue.

"When I told him that was the best we could do, he asked me one thing," said Mitchell, then an assistant general manager for the Redskins. "He asked me how much are the hot dogs. I said, 'Well, Mr. Cooke, I got those down to 50 cents.' And he just loved that. 'That's right! I knew you could negotiate! I knew it!' He

# Hall of Fame

Redskins founder George Preston Marshall was a charter inductee of the Pro Football Hall of Fame in 1963, along with former quarterback Sammy Baugh and Earl "Curly" Lambeau, the longtime coach of the Green Bay Packers who coached Washington in 1952 and 1953. Here's the complete list of the twenty-one Redskins in the Pro Football Hall of Fame:

George Allen, coach (1971–77)
Cliff Battles, running back (1932–37)
Sammy Baugh, quarterback (1937–52)
Bill Dudley, running back (1950–51, 1953)
Turk Edwards, tackle (1932–40)
Ray Flaherty, coach (1937–42)
Joe Gibbs, coach (1981–92)
Otto Graham, coach (1966–68)
Ken Houston, safety (1973–80)
Sam Huff, linebacker (1964–67, 1969)
Deacon Jones, defensive end (1974)
Stan Jones, defensive tackle (1966)
Sonny Jurgensen, quarterback (1964–74)
Paul Krause, safety (1964–67)
Curly Lambeau, coach (1952–53)
Vince Lombardi, coach (1969)
George Preston Marshall, founder (1932–69)
Wayne Millner, end (1936–41, 1945)
Bobby Mitchell, flanker (1962–68)
John Riggins, running back (1976–79, 1981–85)
Charley Taylor, wide receiver (1964–77)

knows there is a price, and you have to make sure you do the full thing. Don't do it partially."

Nobody dared do anything partially under Cooke. He challenged employees, berated them, and even corrected their English. He'd chastise others if they weren't "reading the classics." He'd fret over quotes given to reporters and would call them back, sometimes a few times, to change the quote or improve the wording.

Cooke was demanding, and he intimidated some employees with his force and presence—even from the grave. Longtime trainer Bubba Tyer didn't want to reveal any of his favorite Cooke stories seven years after the owner's death in 1997. Why? Let's just say a fear of ghosts. Cooke often boasted he wasn't going to die, and no one doubted him on anything. That's why Tyer didn't want to divulge the one time Cooke let him have it, upset over something to do with a chair. "I'm not going into that," Tyer said, laughing.

"You were always on your toes when you were around him," Tyer said. "He could be very gracious and pat you on the cheek and say, 'Bubba, Bubba, Bubba. Be a good boy.' Or he could say, 'Why did I ever hire you?' He was the kind of guy—you'd get a kick out of being around him when he was in a good mood. And you ran with your tail between your legs when he was in a bad mood, because he could be great on either end of the spectrum."

There's a reason former Washington mayor Sharon Pratt Kelly referred to Cooke as the "Billionaire Bully" when they were trying to negotiate for a new stadium. On the other hand, when Tyer's predecessor, Joe Kuczo, suffered a massive stroke after retiring, Cooke took care of his insurance and gave him a stipend. After his death, Cooke's estate provided for Kuczo until Kuczo's death in 2003.

In most cases, Cooke's employees stuck around, particularly those making the football decisions. The only time former general manager Charley Casserly would discuss personnel moves with him was before the draft, letting him know whom they were going to take. They'd also discuss their free-agency budget plans. If it was a high-priced player, they'd get clearance from Cooke first. "Mr. Cooke never got involved in trying to make a personnel decision," Casserly said. "He'd get involved in the money part of it. He was very knowledgeable about the basics of running a franchise and he had patience. He could go through tough times. He listened to nobody but his football people, and that was it. When I was there, he listened to Joe [Gibbs] and myself and no one else."

Cooke also liked to spar with his decision makers, testing their convictions about a move. That's why he allowed the team to sign quarterback Doug Williams, slated to be a backup, for a then-high sum of $400,000 in 1986. "He would try to intimidate people," Casserly said. "If you really believed in something and you knew he was dead set against it, you had to fight and win. He would put up a hell of a fight, but at the end of the day if he saw you were convinced on something, he'd let you do it.

"If there was a big contract involved, he'd ask you a lot of questions and he'd make you come back a couple times before he'd let you do something of that magnitude. He was testing you."

And he could tweak his workers. Before the 1991 season, Cooke once told Gibbs that he had screwed up the team, adding, "That Jimmy Johnson down in Dallas knows how to put a team together."

"Sometimes he would say, 'You've got too many old players,'" Gibbs said. "Whatever he felt, he had to say to make a point.

*Owner Jack Kent Cooke, left, running back John Riggins, and head coach Joe Gibbs, right, share the game ball after the Redskins won Super Bowl XVII.* AP

Sometimes that did motivate me. He expected great performances. His favorite saying was, 'You're going to do better than your believed best.' He was more committed to winning than finances. The other thing about him is that he was better when we were at our worst than when it was good." Which is what happened during Gibbs's first season, when the Redskins started 0–5. Cooke called Gibbs to his house and reassured him, giving him a hefty dose of confidence.

Working for Cooke meant fulfilling different duties. Such was the case with former public relations director Rick Vaughn. One day at Redskins Park, Vaughn was asked to do something a little different. As Cooke slowly rode in a golf cart from the front of the facility to the practice fields, Vaughn sat on the back—holding a leash and walking the owner's dog, Coco. As the cart passed by the pressroom, Vaughn looked in, smiled, and shrugged his shoulders.

Cooke bought a 25 percent share in the Redskins in 1962 for $350,000. Eventually, with George Preston Marshall in failing health, his 52 percent share was retired. That meant Cooke became the new majority owner. But, because he also owned the NBA's Los Angeles Lakers and the NHL's Los Angeles Kings, the NFL's cross-ownership rules prohibited him from running the Redskins. In 1979 he sold the other teams, spurred in part by a $42 million divorce settlement, and moved from California to Virginia. He took over the decision making from Edward Bennett Williams.

During Cooke's tenure, the Redskins won three Super Bowls, lost a fourth, and reached the playoffs eight times. He also paid for a new stadium in Landover, Maryland, at a time when other owners sought city or state funds to do so. After his death in April of 1997, it was named for him until new owner Dan Snyder sold the naming rights.

Cooke also became quite the entertainer, using the owner's box to host celebrities and politicians. "He was part showman, part fan during the games," Casserly said. "He would play to the crowd in the box to some degree. But he wanted to win, and if things weren't going well he'd turn around and yell at me. That was just part of the job description. But when the game was over, it was forgotten. I never took it serious."

The game Casserly always will remember is the final home game at RFK against Dallas in December of 1996. Cooke, who would die several months later, was too ill to attend. So Casserly wound up watching into the third quarter of the Redskins' 37–10 victory at Cooke's house in Northwest Washington. "You can bet that I was hoping we'd win that one because there wasn't anyone else for him to talk to," he said. "That's the one I'll always remember. I'm sure he appreciated it. He was the biggest fan."

## Dan Snyder

Dan Snyder charged into the league full of energy and bravado, a new-wave owner ready to topple the game. In 1999, at the Redskins first scrimmage during his tenure, Snyder's entrance illustrated a difference between the so-called old guard and the one promised by him.

Longtime Pittsburgh Steelers owner Dan Rooney walked the track surrounding the football field at Frostburg State University by himself, wearing khakis and a white polo shirt. He blended into the surroundings. A short time later, Snyder's helicopter landed nearby; wearing a dark suit he walked briskly onto the field, followed by several others in dark suits. Good or bad, it represented a difference, and a change.

Snyder's early tenure was anything but successful, save for a division title in 1999 that was put together by the outgoing front office. After sending around a letter telling employees their jobs were safe, Snyder fired many of them. He changed coaches with regularity, considered firing coordinators during the season, and spent lavishly in the off-season. In his mind, everything was designed to bring the Redskins a winner. In critics' minds, he was playing fantasy football.

In 2000 the Redskins became the first team to charge admission to training camp practice, turning Redskins Park into a mini-

Owner Daniel Snyder at a Redskins news conference in December 2000.
Hillery Smith Garrison/AP

circus with games and refreshment booths set up behind portable stands. Snyder's helicopter was a distracting presence during that camp, players said.

Snyder spent $100 million on the 2000 roster, signing aging stars such as Bruce Smith, Deion Sanders, and Mark Carrier. He angered quarterback Brad Johnson, who was coming off a Pro Bowl season, by signing veteran Jeff George. Johnson got some revenge, making sure Larry Centers reached a $250,000 bonus by completing 7 passes to him in the season finale. After starting

6–2, Washington collapsed and lost four of its next five, leading to head coach Norv Turner's firing. Players could hear Snyder yelling at Turner after some losses.

Early on, Snyder would speak to the team after games. After a 1999 win over the Giants, Turner had just told the team not to talk about getting revenge the next week over Philadelphia, which had beaten the Redskins a week earlier. Then Snyder addressed the team, telling them, amid expletives, to "get revenge" on the Eagles. One former long-time coach said it was as if he was trying to mimic Knute Rockne. The national press, and much of the local media, ripped him. The comic strip Tank McNamara awarded him its "Sports Jerk of the Year" in 2000.

Then came a new coach in Marty Schottenheimer, who was fired because of a power struggle after winning eight of eleven games to close 2001, and another new coach in Steve Spurrier, who resigned after two seasons in part because of conflicts with the front office. Not that many players were disappointed.

Several years after taking over the team, Snyder admitted he had made some mistakes. Once he called former general manager Charley Casserly, whom he had fired rather than Turner his first summer, to tell him, "I fired the wrong guy."

Judging by the team's performance, no one would disagree about his mistakes. But his ownership clearly is a work in progress. Snyder always will be aggressive and demanding—it's how he amassed a fortune at such a young age, allowing him to buy the Redskins at thirty-four. He usually gets what he wants, which is how head coach Joe Gibbs ended up back in Washington in 2004.

For now, Snyder has been muzzled by the presence of Gibbs, the one coach the owner has always wanted—except for Spurrier, who was the other coach he always wanted. However, Gibbs won three Super Bowl trophies in his first stint as coach, giving him increased power upon his return. And in the 2004 training camp, Snyder's helicopter was nowhere to be found during practice. Actually, Snyder often wasn't there, remaining as much in the background as possible. More than a few times, Snyder has admitted, "I came on too strong. I made mistakes."

"We've talked at times about what he should do," said Sonny Jurgensen, the Redskins Hall of Fame quarterback who has befriended the owner. "I said, 'Step back, step back. Don't say anything.' When stuff with [former coach Steve] Spurrier happened, I said, 'Stay out of it.' And he did. He thanked me for that. He's been silent since Joe Gibbs has been back here. Gibbs is the president, and he makes the football decisions. That's difficult for Dan. He's smart and he knows how to make money. He knows how to make things successful, and he wants to apply that right here. But it's a different ball game."

Snyder got the players Gibbs wanted. He also installed a players' lounge at Redskins Park, per Gibbs's wishes, and he hasn't overruled his coach. In the past Snyder also allowed certain players, such as Smith and Darrell Green, to come to him with complaints about coaches. With Gibbs, those days have ended. But Snyder won over some players a different way in 2004. When former teammate Rashad Bauman's son died of SIDS on Thanksgiving Day, Snyder volunteered the use of his plane to fly a handful of Redskins to the funeral. He started the Redskins Leadership Council. "Dan has been everything I could ask for," said Gibbs, sincere in his praise.

Others have seen a new Snyder, too. "Dan understands it better now," Jurgensen said. "From the first day he's wanted to win. A lot say they want to win, but he was willing to spend to win. I used to kid him about being impatient and wanting the quick fix. Now he's realized that doesn't work here. He's more settled in. He's decided we have to approach this thing with baby steps instead of, 'It's gonna happen overnight.'"

If nothing else, Snyder has proven he knows business. He was originally part of an ownership group backing Howard Milstein. But Milstein couldn't get the owners' approval. Snyder smartly assumed Milstein's bid and quickly won approval from the other NFL owners. Had Snyder not assumed the bid, the price tag might have increased by $200 million to $1 billion, as others were willing to pay if the Redskins returned to the market.

He expanded the stadium seating, sold the naming rights to the building, and increased the value of the franchise, even as the team stumbled. *Forbes Magazine* estimated the Redskins value at $1.2 billion in 2004, tops among any U.S. sports franchise. In 2000 Deion Sanders had joked that Snyder, in pursuing free agents, was shopping at "Versace while everyone else was at K-Mart."

At his core, Snyder remains a fan. He grew up watching Washington play every Sunday, wearing his now-famous lucky Redskins belt buckle. He's not about to change too much. The one thing he would like to see changed is the Redskins record. Ultimately, that's how Snyder will be judged, too. If the Redskins win, the perception of him will improve. If not, his ways will be lampooned.

Snyder's learned that success in business doesn't equate to success in football—at least not yet, anyway. The lessons do carry over, though. Snyder failed in his first few attempts in business before succeeding. "You just try to outweigh the bad times," he said, "with good times. I love football. After my family, the Redskins are the most important thing in my life."

## The Great Coaches

### George Allen

After a season-opening win in 1971, the corn-ball coach led his players in a postgame cheer, one that drew smirks from some of the longtime players. The doubters watched as other players joined George Allen in celebration, lapping up his hokey ways. "Three cheers for the Redskins!" Allen shouted. "Hip

hip, hooray!" he and his followers bellowed, repeating the line twice more.

Meanwhile, longtime center Len Hauss, refusing to participate, shook his head in amazement, whispering to teammate Walt Rock, a tackle, "Is this ridiculous or what?"

A week later, the same scene played out. The Redskins won. Allen gathered the players for a cheer as Hauss, Rock, and a few others told themselves and each other, "These are grown men." But a funny thing was happening, something that hadn't happened in a long time. The Redskins were becoming a good football team. Enthusiasm around the city was building rapidly. Players were energized like never before. And even those who had held out could no longer help themselves. That soon included Hauss and his cronies, even if it meant jumping into the postgame silliness. "By the fourth week, we were right up in the middle of it and getting caught up in it," Hauss said.

That was the thing about Allen. Eventually he convinced everyone to follow, because if they did, success and fun would follow, too. That was true of the players and of the fans, who had been starving for success. They found success in Allen, who created a hysteria unmatched to that point in the Redskins annals, turning a historical loser into a consistent winner and changing forever how the franchise was viewed. He convinced players that his methods would work, even the ones that made them laugh or wonder.

"He was just a players' coach," Redskins kicker Mark Moseley said. "The big thing about him was he always tried to build confidence in the players. He was always doing something to make us be grateful that we were there. And he'd always tell us to be thankful we were here."

George Allen became head coach of the Redskins in March 1971. AP

Redskins fans were certainly thankful. From 1946 to 1970, Washington posted four winning seasons and never reached the postseason. In Allen's tenure, from 1971 to 1977, the Redskins never had a losing season, and they reached the Super Bowl once and the playoffs five times. "Before he got here, this place was pathetic," said Redskins longtime trainer Bubba Tyer, who arrived with Allen. "There was real excitement here that first year. He used to say, 'Those players don't know what's taking place.' A lot of us didn't know."

It took place because of Allen, who also was among the most colorful figures in Redskins lore. Among his many quirks: his love of milk and ice cream; his breakfast menu, featuring a daily serving of oatmeal, raisin bread, and grapefruit; his constant phone calls, particularly to linebacker Chris Hanburger; and his many, many sayings. And, of course, his hatred of all things Dallas. "He would stand in front of the team and say, 'If I could cut off my finger to help us beat the Cowboys, I would do it. If I could put solid gold on that door frame to help us beat the Cowboys, I would do it,'" Tyer said. "Of course, it wasn't his money. He never spent his own money."

Ah, the Cowboys. Allen's declared enemy, coached by the man—Tom Landry—he liked beating more than any other. No team dominated his thoughts like Dallas. Once, during an off-season day, Allen wandered over to the horseshoe pitch he had put in at Redskins Park. He grabbed a horseshoe and said, "If I make a ringer, we'll beat the Cowboys." He made it, then walked away saying, "Yes, we've got the Cowboys."

There was end Dallas Hickman, whose first name Allen would never utter. There was his refusal to call Dallas–Fort Worth Airport by its full name, which Charley Casserly learned in 1977. Allen wanted Casserly, who arrived that year as an unpaid intern, to go on a scouting trip to see Baylor, Texas Christian University, North Texas State, and Southern Methodist University. "I asked him, 'Where do I fly into?'" Casserly said. "He said, 'Fly into damn Fort Worth Airport.' And I'm thinking, 'Why did he call it damn airport?'"

So he told Allen's secretary to book him a flight into Fort Worth Airport. Her response: There is no such airport. They went back and forth on this until the secretary asked Casserly to repeat the exact instructions. He told her that he was to fly into "damn Fort Worth Airport." Casserly thought it was some kind of joke. "You have to understand," the secretary told him, "he never uses the word Dallas. It's 'the damn Cowboys.'"

What Allen did like were trades, of which he made many. Before his first training camp, he made nineteen trades involving thirty-three players, including a blockbuster with the team he had just left after five seasons, the Los Angeles Rams. In that deal, Allen traded seven draft picks plus linebacker Marlin McKeever for six players. Allen would eventually trade for ten Rams that off-season. But Allen wanted veterans, which is why he traded away every first-round pick, including peddling Washington's 1973 pick twice, a move that earned him a fine. His motto was, "The future is now." It's also why the Redskins became known as "The Over-the-Hill Gang."

"Players had trust in him, and they were able to perform, even though they had problems in the places they'd played before," defensive tackle Diron Talbert said. "He'd make you better because of the way he communicated with you. He respected all of his players to the point where he didn't criticize too much. And he wouldn't let his assistant coaches criticize too much. He let the players be themselves, and that's hard for a lot of coaches."

"I remember my first day in camp [in 1974]," Moseley said. "He called me over and put his arm around me and said, 'I brought you here because I remember what you did for the Oilers against us [in 1971]. All I need is a kicker who can make a couple field goals because we're gonna have a good defense. I think you're that guy. . . . Now beat out the other twelve kickers and the job is yours.' That was his first speech to me. I was so amazed that he even knew who I was. For him to take a few minutes to say something to me meant everything in the world."

Winning meant everything to Allen, who once told his players after a 24–23 loss to lowly New England in 1972, "I would have cut my arm off if it would have made us win that game. No one should get paid. How can you eat? I wish we could play tomorrow. My God! This is losing!"

But Allen didn't lose often, guiding the Redskins to the Super Bowl in his second season. He worked the players hard, routinely keeping them on the field for three hours. And he had simple, but strong beliefs about how to win. "His philosophy was that defense was number one, special teams number two," Hauss said, "and I used to say parking attendants number three, front office number four, cheerleaders number five, and then the offense, if you've got time. But he said you win with defense, and I couldn't prove him wrong."

"I never saw George go in an offensive meeting room," Talbert said. "Maybe just a few times through the years."

Because of Allen's conservative offensive ways, he clashed with longtime Redskins quarterback Sonny Jurgensen, and he favored Billy Kilmer as the offense's caretaker. Once Jurgensen, who entered for an injured Kilmer, ignored a call for a draw on a third down. Instead, Jurgensen called a pass play and threw for a touchdown. When Jurgensen reached the sidelines, Allen demanded to know why he didn't run the draw. Jurgensen told him he heard the defense shouting out, "Watch for the draw!" Jurgensen didn't reenter.

Allen, enshrined in the Hall of Fame in 2002, was always playing mind games. He'd phone Cowboys coach Tom Landry the week of their game just for kicks. He had the hot water turned off in the visiting locker room when Dallas played in Washington in 1971. And he always sought an advantage. He once held a tryout the same weekend as the Super Bowl, boasting to Tyer, "See, we're getting ready for next season; they're still on this season."

Eventually, Allen wore out owner Edward Bennett Williams, who once said the Redskins "gave George an unlimited budget, and he exceeded it." He also said, "We gave him unlimited patience, and he exceeded it."

But because of Allen, the perception of the Redskins changed forever. "The Redskins were already selling out when George came," Casserly said. "But they never had Redskins mania. He created the Redskins mania that exists today."

## Joe Gibbs

Allen may have created that mania, but it was Joe Gibbs who took it to its greatest heights by leading the franchise to three Super Bowl victories. In 2004 Gibbs returned to the sidelines after more than a decade away, once again displaying the personality that made him beloved. Here was the greatest coach in franchise history, the one with the three Super Bowl trophies and a city that

# Career Records

Year-by-year career records for George Allen and Joe Gibbs during their tenures with the Redskins:

| George Allen | | |
|---|---|---|
| **Year** | **Regular Season** | **Playoffs** |
| 1971 | 9–4–1 | (lost first playoff game) |
| 1972 | 11–3–0 | (advanced to Super Bowl VII) |
| 1973 | 10–4–0 | (lost first playoff game) |
| 1974 | 10–4–0 | (lost first playoff game) |
| 1975 | 8–6–0 | |
| 1976 | 10–4–0 | (lost first playoff game) |
| 1977 | 9–5–0 | |
| **Totals** | **67–30–1** | (69–35–1 including postseason) |

| Joe Gibbs | | |
|---|---|---|
| **Year** | **Regular Season** | **Playoffs** |
| 1981 | 8–8–0 | |
| 1982 | 8–1–0 | (won Super Bowl XVII) |
| 1983 | 14–2–0 | (advanced to Super Bowl XVIII) |
| 1984 | 11–5–0 | (lost first playoff game) |
| 1985 | 10–6–0 | |
| 1986 | 12–4–0 | (adv. to NFC Championship Game) |
| 1987 | 11–4–0 | (won Super Bowl XXII) |
| 1988 | 7–9–0 | |
| 1989 | 10–6–0 | |
| 1990 | 10–6–0 | (advanced to divisional playoffs) |
| 1991 | 14–2–0 | (won Super Bowl XXVI) |
| 1992 | 9–7–0 | (advanced to divisional playoffs) |
| 2004 | 6–10–0 | |
| **Totals** | **130–70–0** | (146–75–0 including postseason) |

adored his every step and considered him a coaching genius, standing amid a group of reporters after practice that year and talking about . . . "The Wizard of Id" and *Young Frankenstein.*

The latter he dubbed the "greatest movie to come down the pike" before repeating a conversation from the film: "Let me get this right. I put an abnormal brain in a 9-foot-tall body? I'm gonna kill you!" And of the comic strip he says, "I like that little guy," repeating the words from one strip that summed up his thoughts on his role compared to the players': "The wizard is sitting on a horse with the King, and the little foot soldier says, 'Are you going to be in your usual place during the charge?' He says, 'Yes.' The soldier says, 'Then we'll keep the dust down.'"

Reporters cracked up, first because it was funny and second because, well, Gibbs is a Hall of Fame football coach. Are coaches supposed to act like this? But Gibbs constantly reveals a part of his character, showing why he's beloved by his admirers. He's not just a football coach. He's like one of them, they figure.

Gibbs showed that side a month earlier in the 2004 training camp. After one practice, Gibbs excused himself from a press gathering to ask a group of passing fans, which included some in wheelchairs, if they wanted him to sign anything. Gibbs had already spent thirty minutes signing autographs for VIPs, but he did not remember signing any for this group. So he hopped off the riser and spent the next five minutes signing, with one fan telling him, "My dad would be tickled to death to see this."

More than most coaches, Gibbs isn't afraid to present other sides of his personality, allowing people to warm to him, especially the fans. But that's not the only reason they love him. Those three trophies sitting in the lobby at Redskins Park have something to do with their affection, too. That's why the area celebrated for months when he announced his return after eleven seasons, a retirement forced for health reasons (diabetes) and burnout. He also had nothing left to prove.

It's debatable who is the best coach in NFL history, but this point can't be argued: Gibbs is the only coach in history to win a Super Bowl with three different quarterbacks, none of whom will enter the Hall of Fame. So far the only player to reach the Hall of Fame from those days is running back John Riggins, who played on only one Super Bowl win for Gibbs. But to Houston general manager Charley Casserly, any argument about the best coach begins and ends with Gibbs. Casserly worked with Gibbs for twelve years, first as an assistant general manager and then as the general manager.

"He was an innovator on offense," Casserly said. "He was a master strategist, and the thing he could do was figure out what each player could do, what would work, and how to get them to execute it, and the idea of using multiple formations and shifting and motion to disguise plays. No one did it better than he did. When you look at the St. Louis and Kansas City offenses of today, that's where it comes from. And he was a great tactician, a great motivator. He had a tremendous ability to adjust, not only during the game but from season to season."

Gibbs's résumé is well known: a .683 winning percentage entering the 2004 season—best all-time among coaches with more than 125 wins—and a spot in the Pro Football Hall of Fame. And he's the only one who has returned to the place where he developed his reputation. There's a reason Washington was so excited that he returned: The Redskins were 74–101–1 under the five coaches who followed Gibbs.

But winning has followed Gibbs most of his life. After leaving

Washington, Gibbs became a successful NASCAR owner. He is also a former senior national racquetball champion. "He's cutthroat competitive," said his son Coy, a member of his new staff. "We could be water-skiing, Jet Skiing. My mom is just as competitive. It's a crazy family, my mom, dad, brother, and me. We go at it, whether it's Monopoly or swimming, Jet Skis, whatever we're doing. If my dad loses at Monopoly, there's anger, oh yeah. It doesn't matter whether it's Monopoly or a football game. The guy's going for it."

That anger rarely surfaces. When it does, the players know it's serious. Once, during a sloppy practice, Gibbs ordered his players into a team meeting. Then he punched an overhead projector, letting his players know such practices wouldn't be tolerated. "He didn't cuss, but he was beet red and said, 'All right, we'll try this one more time, and we'll go out there and we'll get practice right,'" said former Redskins tight end Donnie Warren. "It took us about four and a half hours to complete practice."

Another story comes courtesy of longtime assistant Joe Bugel: "One time in Philly, we're behind at halftime, and we stunk up the joint. He came in and his face was red and the big vein is sticking out of his neck. He started clearing Gatorade off the tables. He's throwing oranges. He's screaming so hard, I said I'd better get ready. I thought I was going to have to give him mouth to mouth. . . . We went out and kicked their rear ends."

And one more from Bugel: "We're at the Super Bowl for the first time and everybody's supposed to ride on the bus. The coaches got lost, everyone's late. And he whacked the overhead, broke it, and it shattered. He split his hand and said, 'I want everyone to ride the bus, coaches included. We're not going to start off like this!' We knew he was serious then. Joe isn't a screamer, but you know when he's mad."

What Gibbs didn't do, and still doesn't, is criticize his players in public. He's fiercely loyal and saves the hard talks for private. Instead, Gibbs made the players fear him, or what he might do to their careers. "We're in a meeting once at summer camp and we had nine tight ends there," Warren said. "He told all of us, 'One thing I can put up with are physical mistakes as far as you dropping a pass. But a mental mistake where you miss a cornerback coming on a blitz and he hits our quarterback and he fumbles the ball and we lose or he gets hurt . . . Guess what? You're out of here. You should know that stuff.' And it happened. We had a situation where a guy hits the quarterback, he fumbles. The following Monday—it was a preseason game—we come back, and that tight end is gone. It starts to make you think."

Motivating players became one of Gibbs's strengths. Former Redskins safety Brad Edwards remembers struggling as a reserve rookie, only to have Gibbs tell him he wasn't playing the way he expected, and that he could do better. Edwards, who went on to become a starter the next season, has called that "leadership at its finest."

For Warren, who played in Washington from 1979 to 1992 and retired rather than play for another head coach, the motivation came in what wasn't said. "Joe might have come up to me two times and said, 'You know what, Donnie? You played one hell of a game,'" Warren said. "What does that do to a player after other games? In the back of my mind, I know I played well. Is he going to come up to me and tell me I played well? He didn't. So I'm going, 'Holy shit, maybe I didn't play that well. Maybe I need to do better.' That's what drove me. But Joe treated everyone different, and he knew everyone's personality."

Gibbs's first speech to the team in 1981 focused on how he

*Head coach Joe Gibbs shares a laugh with quarterback Mark Brunell before a game in 2004.* Evan Vucci/AP

wanted people with character—and that of the 130 or so in attendance, nearly 100 would be cut. "That woke everyone up," said
former Redskins kicker Mark Moseley. "I bought into it real hard.
He said, 'We'll have the best people, the best secretaries, the best
players. We're going to win because we want the best people.' I use
that in my speeches all the time. That had so much impact on me."

"If you pick the right people," Gibbs said, "they make you look
good. And you never embarrass someone in front of his peers. You
talk one-on-one if it's serious. Some people you have to get on.

# Tricks of the Trade

After Joe Gibbs initially retired following the 1992 season, the Redskins went through five coaches over the next eleven years. The last was Steve Spurrier, a highly successful college coach who won only twelve of thirty-two games for Washington from 2002 to 2003.

Everyone knows Spurrier cared first and foremost about the offense. That was evident one day in his second training camp. As the first-team defense worked against the scout-team offense, Spurrier stood off to the side with the kickers, ignoring the action. Instead, he was showing the kickers how he could bounce the ball on the ground and catch it behind his back.

Some you have to give them a little sugar, and they'll die for you."

Late-night coaching sessions became commonplace as Gibbs often slept on a cot in his office. Some reporters who covered the team under Gibbs in his first stint joked that he had to stay late because he'd spend so much time telling stories well past the dinner hour. But Gibbs liked to work the late shift, downing a candy bar (or three) and getting to work. It wasn't good for his health, but it was good for the Redskins. Interestingly, Gibbs is healthier now, but his work ethic hasn't changed.

"Being able to stay up eighteen straight hours without batting an eye," said Bugel, an assistant from 1981 to 1989 and again now, "working on a game plan to put everyone in the best possible position, that's toughness to me. He left no stone unturned, and there was a trickle-down effect. When you see the coaches with bags under their eyes and they're still enthusiastic, the players say, 'If they can work all night, why can't we?'"

Not everything has been golden for Gibbs. He was the offensive coordinator of a Tampa Bay team that won only five games in 1978. There was his diabetes, brought on, he believes, by his shoddy diet. And he filed for bankruptcy in the mid-1980s, the result of a failed investment after he had cosigned a loan. "I put me and my family on the brink of losing everything," Gibbs said. "At that point I thought it was going to hit the papers and I'd be the laughingstock of the world. It was four years of misery. Financially, I was a mess."

But he recovered by sticking to his core beliefs, which revolve around religion. "For me it's just the basics, and that's what the Bible preaches," Gibbs said. "I believe in those concepts. There's a game plan for life, and we need to study it. Every time I get outside that game plan, I get squished."

As Gibbs talked about this, he again showed his funny bone, a word he loves to use. After detailing his failures, which he said were all in a book he once wrote, one reporter jokingly asked, "How did you get this job then?"

"[Owner Dan Snyder] didn't read the book," Gibbs joked. "I didn't give it to him until afterward."

Gibbs knows how hard it is returning to the scene of his greatest triumphs. There's no guarantee things will turn out the same way. But he wanted to return, and Washington was the only place he would coach. "It's probably one of the toughest deals you could imagine," Gibbs said. "Part of that is the thrill of saying that it's hard and getting a chance to do it."

Others know why he did it, all of them having watched the franchise slide in his absence. "He came back for one reason," Bugel said, "to win a Super Bowl. He came to get the program back."

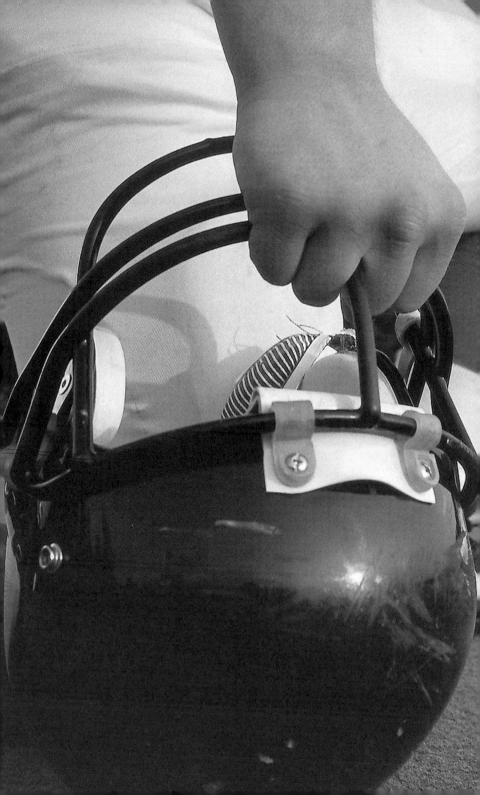

# Super Finishes

The Redskins, and especially their fans, endured more than two decades of futility. Not only did they fail to make the playoffs from 1945 to 1970, they rarely even posted a winning record. Calling themselves champions was too laughable to consider.

That changed when George Allen became coach in 1971, and the Redskins appeared in a Super Bowl one year later. But it wasn't until another decade passed that

Washington could claim NFL supremacy. And by the time another ten years passed, the Redskins would challenge for the title of Best Team of the Decade. With three Super Bowl titles, and a fourth appearance, it was a period unmatched in Redskins history.

## Super Bowl XVII

As the Redskins stretched during a practice the week of Super Bowl XVII, running back John Riggins called Don Breaux over, the running backs coach. He quietly posed a question, revealing his intentions. All Breaux could do was smile.

"Don, what's the Super Bowl rushing record?" Riggins asked.

"John, I don't have any idea but I'll find out for you," Breaux said.

He found out the record and delivered the news to Riggins: Franco Harris had rushed for 158 yards in Super Bowl IX. "That pointed out to me that he was thinking about doing something great," Breaux said. And Breaux waited for the response he knew would come on the field.

And it did, not only from Riggins but also from the rest of his teammates in this 27–17 win over Miami. Washington had waited a long time for this victory, since 1942 when it won an NFL championship. Since that time the Redskins had endured long stretches of futility, followed by a decade of success in the 1970s. But they lost to Miami in Super Bowl VII and hadn't won another playoff game until the 1982 season.

Coach Joe Gibbs had changed their fortunes, but no one predicted that would happen after an 0–5 start his first season. After the fifth loss, and an all-night coaches' meeting, he scrapped the two-back set with John Riggins and Joe Washington, neither of whom wanted to block, and used a one-back formation that became his trademark. More points and wins followed as the Redskins rallied to an 8–8 record.

The players didn't lose confidence in the staff during this stretch, laying a strong base for the future. "The attention to detail was unparalleled," said former tight end Rick "Doc" Walker. "They made the game fun and it was all based off the premise that you fight first."

"It was tough," said former field-goal kicker Mark Moseley. "But when we'd come in Monday after a defeat, he would come back in and say, 'Keep believing. . . . and eventually we'll win.'"

That happened in 1982, a season in which a players' strike reduced the regular season to nine games. Washington lost only once, then rolled through the playoffs with wins over Detroit, Minnesota, and hated Dallas. A week later in Pasadena, California, the Redskins faced Miami.

Washington lacked a lot of star power as a number of key players had originally entered the NFL as undrafted free agents. But the Redskins did have a few standouts—Riggins, Moseley, quarterback Joe Theismann, receiver Art Monk—as well as some players who eventually would become big names, like defensive end Dexter Manley, a fifth-round pick from Oklahoma State in 1981. He would go on to become the Redskins all-time leading sacker with 97.5, but he would also battle drug and alcohol problems.

This season, however, Manley was a rising standout on an excellent defense. In the NFC Championship Game, he knocked out Dallas quarterback Danny White and he deflected a pass that defensive tackle Darryl Grant intercepted and returned for a touchdown. "He was a fun-loving guy," Grant said.

"We were both from Texas so we bonded. He was a good guy. I kept him in line as much as I could on the field and reminded him what calls were made and what adjustments were necessary. I didn't see his problems coming. I didn't pay close attention until an incident in Georgetown. Then there were a couple other episodes, and it became apparent there was a situation. He was definitely headed on a path to the Hall of Fame."

Maybe. But he was part of a defense that confounded Miami in the Super Bowl. A Manley sack forced a fumble that led to Washington's first points, a 31-yard Moseley field goal. The Dolphins, though, already had scored on a 76-yard pass. They made it 10–3 when Fulton Walker set up a 20-yard field goal with a 42-yard kickoff return. But the Redskins tied it in the second quarter when Theismann hit receiver Alvin Garrett in the corner of the end zone.

The tie didn't last long as Walker returned the ensuing kickoff 98 yards for a score with fewer than two minutes left in the first half. But the Dolphins wouldn't score again, gaining only 2 first downs in the second half.

However, Theismann made the biggest defensive play in the game. Trailing 17–13 and starting from his own 18, Theismann threw a pass into the right flat. Miami linebacker Kim Bokamper tipped it up and was about to grab it inside the 10, and probably score, when Theismann swatted the ball out of his hands.

Eventually this game returned to Riggins. On fourth and 1 from the Miami 43 late in the game, the Redskins called a Riggins run off left tackle. The only problem was Miami's alignment, as the Dolphins used a six-man front. If everyone is blocked, a big play is possible. If not, then it's stuffed.

The Redskins celebrate a touchdown during Super Bowl XVII on January 30, 1983 against the Miami Dolphins. AP

Left tackle Joe Jacoby had to create the opening by eliminating Bokamper. That proved to be no problem. Not that Jacoby knew what happened after he'd made his block. "I didn't see it," Jacoby said. "I was down on the bottom of a pile. . . . But we hitched up to John and he carried us through that. It was just a matter of time."

Blocking back Otis Wonsley helped seal the end, and only Miami corner Don McNeal had a shot. But Riggins swatted away his arm-tackle attempt as if it were a fly. He didn't stop running until he crossed the end zone. "The beautiful thing about Riggo is that he'd just bust guys' arms in the process," Doc Walker said. "Next thing you know you hear those diesel horns going. It's over."

After forcing another three-and-out, the Redskins drove for the clinching score. Riggins helped move the Redskins from the Miami 43 to the 6. From there Theismann and Brown hooked up for a touchdown.

Riggins finished with a Super Bowl–record 166 yards rushing. After the game and after a congratulatory phone call from President Ronald Reagan, Riggins said, "At least for tonight, Ron's the president, but I'm the king." The president was also among the well-wishers later that night at Dulles Airport.

But it wasn't just Riggins who felt good. "We always took a rap for not having a bunch of superstars," Grant said. "But we had football players who were smart and knew what they had to do and they got the job done. To be part of the first Super Bowl team with the Redskins is real cool."

# Super Bowl XXII

The night before the biggest game of their lives, quarterback Doug Williams sat in a dentist's chair undergoing root canal surgery; running back Timmy Smith wondered if he was going to start. Had Smith been told any earlier, he knows what would have happened. "I would have thrown up," he said later.

The Redskins didn't want to scare their improving rookie fifth-round pick from Texas Tech, one coming off a 72-yard performance in the NFC Championship Game win over Minnesota. But the coaches knew all week that they'd start Smith ahead of George Rogers. And the coaches knew that Smith probably had figured it out as well. Even the wise veteran Williams knew that would happen, so he told teammate Darryl Grant before the team arrived in San Diego to "hang out with Timmy and make sure he's cool."

"We babysat him the whole way down there," Grant said. "We'd get the limo out when we'd go to dinner just to make sure everything was straight."

Meanwhile Williams's mind was preoccupied with the pain in his mouth (and not his becoming the first African-American to start at quarterback in the Super Bowl). Root canal surgery has come a long way, but in January 1988 it was still a lengthy, sometimes painful process—in this case, one that lasted three and a half hours. "The job at hand was to win a Super Bowl," Williams said. "Doug Williams's jaw pain wasn't as important as the rest of the team. If you're going to play, you had to do something."

Maybe this would cause Williams to not be as sharp. Maybe Smith would not be able to handle the pressure of starting. Those were legitimate questions. But by the end of this game, one ques-

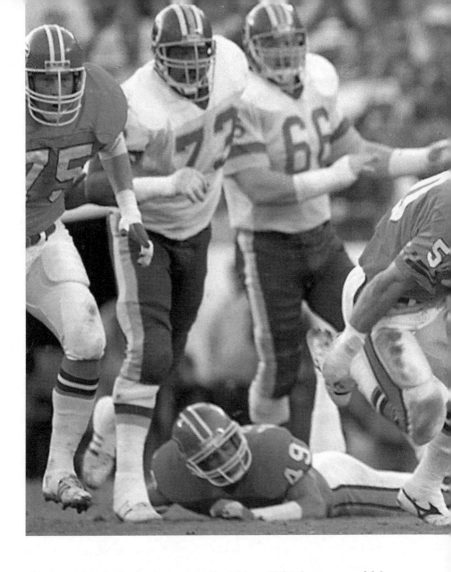

tion remained about these two Redskins: Which one would be named MVP?

Williams put on the best one-quarter display of passing in Super Bowl history. When the second quarter began, Washington trailed 10–0. In fewer than six minutes the Redskins

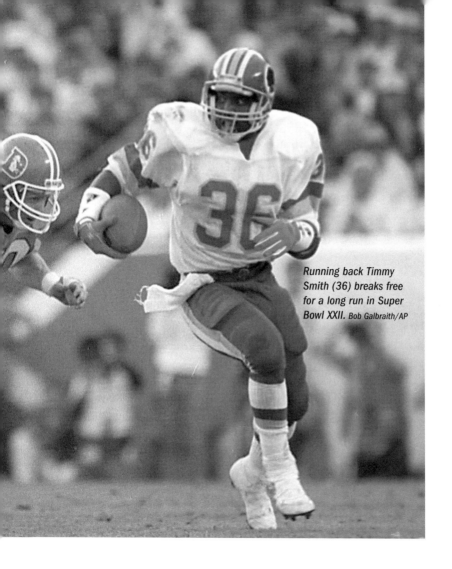

Running back Timmy Smith (36) breaks free for a long run in Super Bowl XXII. Bob Galbraith/AP

exploded for 35 points, thanks to Williams's passing and Smith's running. During this scoring outburst, Williams passed for 228 yards while Smith rushed for 122. "No one has had a quarter like that in history," Williams said. "In a game like that, one person can't be in a zone. All cylinders have to work, which means everyone else was in a zone, too."

First, though, John Elway's heroics gave Denver short-lived hope. He passed 56 yards to receiver Ricky Nattiel for a touchdown on the Broncos' first play from scrimmage. One series later he caught a pass from running back Steve Sewell setting up a field goal.

Ironically, the Redskins prepared for that play all week. But Denver had run it the opposite way in previous games. When the Redskins practiced it, they always ran it toward end Dexter Manley's side. His tip-off would be Elway lining up in shotgun formation. As a reminder, end Charles Mann would shout out "shotgun!" to alert Manley to the possibility of a throwback. Mann spent all week doing this. But when it came to the game, Denver ran it at Mann. "As I look for the receiver, Elway ran past me," Mann said. "Then I look at Sewell running with the ball the other way. Then it hit me. Elway went three or four steps past me and I said, 'Oh, no!'"

Fortunately for Mann, safety Alvin Walton tackled Elway around the 10 yard line. Another thing happened after this series: The defensive players changed their cleats. "We were slipping and sliding everywhere," Mann said. "They had put all that paint on the field. We went to longer spikes and the rest is history. While we're changing cleats, Doug Williams was putting [it] to them. And Ricky Sanders. And Timmy Smith. It was just phenomenal."

First came an 80-yard touchdown pass to receiver Sanders, who adjusted to the defense and ran a fly route instead of a hitch. On the next series, Williams connected with receiver Gary Clark for a 27-yard score and 14–10 lead.

Then it was Smith's turn. It was supposed to be a counter run to the right. But rather than step left and go right, Smith actually first stepped right and then left before realizing his mistake and cutting the other way again. "Doug handed the ball off and slapped him on the butt," running backs coach Don Breaux said. "Timmy had started the wrong way."

Didn't matter. Smith took it 58 yards for a touchdown. After the defense forced another three and out, Williams needed only three plays, the last a 50-yard strike to Sanders, to make it 28–10. Finally, Smith and Williams combined for another touchdown. First Smith gained 43 yards on a run, setting up an eventual 8-yard pass to tight end Clint Didier.

And then it was complete, the Redskins' greatest quarter. Smith punctuated the 42–10 win with a 4-yard run in the fourth quarter. On the sidelines Smith and Sanders debated which one of them would win the MVP. Both made a strong case, setting Super Bowl records for yardage: Smith had rushed for 204 yards; Sanders had caught 8 passes for 190 yards. The defense helped out, too, as corner Barry Wilburn intercepted 2 passes after picking off 9 during the regular season, and Walton had 2 of the Redskins' 5 sacks. But the award went to Williams, who completed 18 of 29 passes for a Super Bowl–record 331 yards.

In reality, the coaching staff and front office also deserved special mention. Earlier that season, a players' strike wiped out one game and forced three others to be played with replacement players. The Redskins, led by assistant general manager Charley Casserly, had a list of players ready. They used eighteen players who had been in their camp that summer. They also had an ex-con and a security guard from a 7-11 in Washington, D.C.

New York certainly wasn't prepared. The Giants had defeated Washington three times the previous year, but when the strike ended they were 0–5 compared to the Redskins' 4–1 record. Washington's mark included a 13–7 win over Dallas, in

# Super Teams

The Redskins are one of only seven NFL franchises to win as many as three Super Bowls. The clubs that have won multiple Super Bowl championships are:

| Team | Record in the Super Bowl |
|---|---|
| San Francisco 49ers | 5–0 |
| Dallas Cowboys | 5–3 |
| Pittsburgh Steelers | 4–1 |
| Green Bay Packers | 3–1 |
| Oakland/L.A. Raiders | 3–2 |
| Washington Redskins | 3–2 |
| New England Patriots | 3–2 |
| New York Giants | 2–1 |
| Miami Dolphins | 2–3 |
| Denver Broncos | 2–4 |

which eleven Cowboy regulars, including quarterback Danny White and running back Tony Dorsett, played.

The strike wasn't easy. Grant smashed a window with his hand as the bus carrying replacement players reached Redskins Park for their first practice. But that was the only violence as the coaches and front office stressed staying united. "It was the only time in the NFL that I didn't want to go to work," Casserly said. "I remember walking in one day talking to one of the players, and he was bitching about the [replacement] players in here. I said, 'Let me tell you something, we've got three division games in a row. We don't know when you're coming back and these games count. We have to do our job right now. You do your job and let's figure out where this is at the end.'"

At the end the strike players helped Washington to an 8–1 record, which helped them host Minnesota in the NFC Championship Game and which also helped them win when the game came down to the final play. And that led them to Denver, whom the players felt never had a chance. "Denver was more of a finesse team and we were a power team," Williams said. "We realized that sooner or later, once all the trickery was over with, they had to play football. And there was no doubt we had the best team."

## Super Bowl XXVI

They detected signs early in the season, clues for a promising season: a blowout in the opener when the other team's star running back can't play; a stirring comeback in the second game, a Monday nighter at their hated rival, Dallas. Watching those games and knowing what he had on the roster prompted defensive coordinator Richie Petitbon to make a declaration.

"We're in the locker room after the Dallas game and he said, 'We're going to the Super Bowl,'" running back Earnest Byner said. "You hear it, but you don't pay attention to it. It was a great game, back and forth. But when he said that, you're thinking, 'OK, really?' But then those things start to happen . . . and we're like, 'Hey, what else can happen?'"

What else can happen? They can play a Philadelphia team missing its top two quarterbacks, starter Randall Cunningham and Jim McMahon. They can watch a usually reliable Houston kicker miss a 34-yarder late in regulation, allowing them to win in overtime.

But the Redskins also won big, posting three shutouts in the first five games. The Redskins won their first eleven games before Dallas beat them, and they caught another break when Detroit upset Dallas to reach the NFC Championship Game. The Cowboys had given Washington its toughest games, also losing 33–31 (blowing a 21–10 lead). In a rematch of a 45–0 win in the season opener, Detroit again offered little challenge and the Redskins won 41–10. "That whole year was a great year," defensive end Charles Mann said.

It was a year in which a 24–7 win over Atlanta in the second round of the playoffs provided a memorable scene. Falcons coach Jerry Glanville incensed Washington when, surrounded by his players, he held a Redskins helmet aloft at midfield before the game. The Redskins had beaten them 56–17 earlier in the season and were taken aback by Atlanta's attitude. "You're thinking, 'This guy is a lunatic,'" Redskins tackle Joe Jacoby said.

The fans thought the same—and worse. So when Washington put the game out of reach with 6:32 remaining on a Gerald Riggs touchdown run, thousands of yellow seat cushions—a giveaway item on this January day—rained onto the field. Jacoby owns a picture of the scene, which hangs on his basement wall: He's sitting in the mud after Riggs scored with a smile on his face and his arms raised. "All of a sudden I look up and see those yellow things flying down," Jacoby said. "I'm lucky I had my helmet on. The fans were paying Mr. Glanville some respect. We rubbed it back in his face."

It was also a year in which coach Joe Gibbs allowed his veterans more say. A group of players, including Mann, Jacoby, Russ Grimm, Jim Lachey, Monte Coleman, and Art Monk, would see Gibbs with any problems they might have. Once they asked him about getting an extra day off. Gibbs agreed—if they won. "It empowered us, like we had broken him down," Mann recalled. "That's not what happened. He was playing us."

But it was also a year in which faith played a larger role on the team. Gibbs's religious preferences were well-known, and it was long whispered that some players carried Bibles around simply to impress him. Or to keep a roster spot. "Gibbs took a lot of heat over the years that he would keep the Christian player longer than a non-Christian," said Mann, himself a Christian, "which I don't think is true. But he knew the Christian player and what commitment that guy had made."

More than anything, they had faith in themselves against Buffalo, playing its second straight Super Bowl. "They had Thurman Thomas and Bruce Smith and Daryl Talley and Andre Reed and Jim Kelly," Mann said. "These guys were awesome. We had a bunch of blue-collar guys. But we knew we were as good or better. Bruce and them were arguing about who was going to say they're going to Disneyland and who would be MVP. That leaked back to our camp. Most of the questions I answered were, 'So tell me about the Christian thing in sports.' We had the 700 Club asking us questions. We spent more time talking about that stuff than who's gonna win the game."

The Bills might have had bigger names, but the Redskins had huge years, which is why eight of them made the Pro Bowl. Quarterback Mark Rypien was named UPI Offensive Player of the Year after throwing 28 touchdowns and 11 interceptions during the regular season. He was in stark contrast to Buffalo quarterback Kelly. The night before the game, Rypien was in his

*Joe Gibbs, surrounded by his players, holds the Vince Lombardi trophy aloft after the Redskins victory in Super Bowl XXVI.* Doug Mills/AP

hotel room with his family. Kelly was in his hotel room with his advisers, mapping out a post–Super Bowl endorsement strategy. Perhaps that typified both teams.

The Redskins blew two scoring opportunities in the first quarter, thanks to a fumbled snap on a field-goal attempt and an interception inside the 10 yard line. But they erupted for 17 second-quarter points, the last 7 points set up by a Darrell Green interception.

The first touchdown came on a 10-yard Rypien-to-Byner pass for a 10–0 lead. Byner had been through his own disastrous post-seasons in Cleveland. He played on the team that watched John Elway drive 98 yards for a tying score as Denver won the AFC Championship in overtime. The following year, after playing a terrific game, Byner fumbled as he was about to score the tying touchdown late in an AFC Championship loss at Denver. Four years later Byner had regained his status as a top back with Washington. "The season was important to me because I was part of a championship team," he said. "And that was it. It didn't bury anything else."

But the Redskins kept burying Buffalo, taking a 17–0 halftime lead. Then, on the first play of the second half, linebacker Kurt Gouveia intercepted Kelly at the Bills' 23, returning it to the 2. Riggs scored for a 24–0 lead.

After Buffalo scored 10 straight points, Rypien hit receiver Gary Clark for a 30-yard score in the third. Eventually the lead grew to 37–10 before Buffalo scored 2 late touchdowns as Washington won 37–24 for its third Super Bowl victory in ten seasons. Rypien was named Super Bowl MVP after passing for 292 yards and 2 touchdowns. He started the year as a holdout, missing the first ten days of training camp. He ended as a major reason why the Redskins won. That's how it went for Washington. "Everything just fell into place," Byner said. "It was a dream season."

# Bitter Rivals

The rivalry started with a few pranks, grown men plotting humorous revenge for slights real and imagined. When Dallas first entered the NFL, the Redskins tried to deny their entry for a year, until Cowboys owner Clint Murchison bought the rights to "Hail to the Redskins." He would return those rights to the Redskins, in exchange for a vote. Suddenly Dallas was in the NFL, placed in the Redskins' division.

# Washington versus Dallas

All-time record, Dallas: 54–32–2

Most points scored, Washington: 41 (1986, 41–14)

Most points scored, Dallas: 45 (1970, 45–21)

Biggest margin of victory, Washington: 27 (1986, 41–14, and
   1996, 37–10)

Biggest margin of victory, Dallas: 35 (1993, 38–3)

Longest winning streak, Washington: 4 (1986–88)

Longest winning streak, Dallas: 10 (1997–2002)

But initially the rivalry was nothing more than a series of behind-the-scenes gags. Some of Murchison's friends once plotted to let loose a bunch of chickens at halftime during a game in Washington, designed to scare dogs carrying Santa Claus's sleigh. Moments before the chickens were to be let loose, the plot was foiled.

The rivalry certainly wasn't anything the rest of the country cared about. Maybe not even the players, who certainly had no reason to hate the other side. Until Dallas started winning, that is. And until George Allen became the Redskins coach in 1971. Then it got serious, and for the next twenty or so years, few NFL rivalries could match this one. It became America's Team versus America's Capital. Cowboys versus Indians.

"It was the contrasting styles of the organization," said former Redskins general manager Charley Casserly, who arrived in 1977 and spent twenty-three seasons in Washington. "The Cowboys were all about glitz. They had the new stadium and rich people sitting there. They were the ones with the big self-promoters. Everything was fancy about them. The Redskins played in an old stadium and were a blue-collar team. There was no trumpeting the horns. These were common people. That's the way we looked at ourselves."

Suddenly, this game mattered greatly in both cities. Eventually, the rest of the country watched with terrific interest, knowing what rested on the outcome. Often it meant a divisional title, or more. Twice it meant a trip to the Super Bowl. Both times the Redskins won those games.

Allen fueled the rise of the rivalry, often reminding his players how Dallas landed in the Redskins' division. His theory: The NFL had provided Dallas extra breaks to help them succeed, owing to a friendship between NFL commissioner Pete Rozelle and Cowboys president Tex Schramm, a member of the NFL's competition committee.

Mostly, though, Allen knew that to make the playoffs, the Redskins would have to unseat Dallas, which had become a consistent winner. It worked. In the four years before Allen's arrival, Washington was 1–7 against Dallas; in Allen's seven seasons the Redskins went 7–8, including one playoff win. Allen even made it personal with Cowboys coach Tom Landry. Before the 1972 NFC Championship Game, Allen told his players, "If I could do this, it would be just me and Tom Landry at the fifty duking it out if that meant the game." Another time Allen dragged a laundry bag around at practice, telling his players, "I know you want to know what's in this bag. It's Tom Landry in the bag. I'm going to drag him around all day like we will on Sunday."

The stoic Landry didn't engage in such behavior, but one of his former players, safety Cliff Harris, once said, "You could tell that it upset him at times." Landry became paranoid that Allen was spying on the Cowboys, assigning guards to stand watch in a hotel across the street from Dallas's practice facility. When a heli-copter would fly overhead, Cowboys players joked that Allen, or one of his employees, was in it. "One elderly lady was in the hotel taking pictures, and the guards went in there and took her film," Dallas running back Tony Dorsett recalled.

Then there was the hype, as Allen encouraged defensive tackle Diron Talbert to engage in verbal warfare, aiming his supposed venom at Dallas quarterback Roger Staubach. Talbert loved to needle Staubach. After Dallas rallied to beat Washington on a last-minute touchdown pass on Thanksgiving Day by reserve quarter-back Clint Longley in 1974—a loss that still haunts Redskins fans—Talbert said, "Clint may be the best quarterback they've got."

Another time, Talbert and Staubach were among the captains representing their teams. At the coin toss, Talbert shook everyone's hand but Staubach's. After Staubach turned away, Talbert half-heartedly stuck out his hand, knowing the gesture wouldn't be returned and that Staubach would be seen as the bad guy. Sure enough, he was—one article called Staubach a poor sport.

Allen would fan these flames, huddling with Talbert during the week to plan what he would say. Inevitably Talbert would say, "We're going to knock him out." Headlines followed. During a postseason banquet in the mid-1970s, Talbert and Staubach bumped into one another, and the Cowboys quarterback asked him, "Why do you hate me so much? I don't hate you." To which Talbert just laughed.

Never mind that it was all an act. Or that they became friends after football. "It was all part of the game, all part of the hype," Talbert said. "It was a big rivalry, and I wish it would get that big again. Right now it's down to nothing. The game isn't as fun to watch without someone not liking someone else for a couple

*Linebacker Ken Harvey (57) sacks Dallas quarterback Troy Aikman (8) in a 1996 game.* Tim Sharp/AP

hours. In the old games, it was serious. The whole week people put up signs in the windows in every store, 'Kill the Cowboys!' All up and down the bars in D.C."

When Allen left following the 1977 season, some of the rivalry's spice evaporated. But not much. By that time, there was too much history, which also furthered the fans' passion, and the rivalry refused to die. Besides, both teams remained among the best in the NFC.

And the players hadn't forgotten allegations of cheap shots by both sides. The Redskins once accused Dallas receiver Lance Alworth of trying to hurt linebacker Jack Pardee with a crackback block. Dallas was incensed when receiver Charley Taylor threw one of his own, injuring Cowboys linebacker Chuck Howley for the season. Dallas called it a cheap shot; Taylor called it part of the game.

Dallas didn't like the Redskins' brash young quarterback, Joe Theismann, and accused him of taunting at the end of one win. Theismann denied it. After a 1979 win in the season finale ended Washington's playoff hopes, Cowboys end Harvey Martin walked a funeral wreath over to the Redskins locker room.

In the 1980s it became Dallas's "Doomsday Defense" against Washington's "Hogs," and Landry against Joe Gibbs, two of the NFL's best. Redskins guard Mark May and Dallas defensive lineman Randy White grew to despise one another, despite rarely being matched one-on-one. May recalled White running at him after plays, then flipping him off. During a mid-1980s seminar where both players represented their teams, White arrived late and found only one chair open. It was next to May. White stood.

On the morning of the biggest game of their lives, the 1972 NFC Championship Game, Billy Kilmer and a few of his teammates got together for breakfast. As the players drank coffee and chatted, Kilmer couldn't believe what was in the newspaper. In black and white, Kilmer read a quote from Dallas coach Tom Landry that provided him with an extra dose of motivation. As if it were needed. "Landry made a statement that the reason they were going to win was because Roger Staubach was a better athlete than Billy Kilmer," he said. "That incensed me. I was ready to go right then."

Truth be told, Kilmer and the Redskins didn't need any extra energy for the game. They certainly didn't need to hear about a supposed slight in the paper to get them riled up for Dallas. They'd been waiting a couple years for this moment, and Redskins fans had waited even longer—like since 1945, the last time Washington had played in a championship game.

But when George Allen arrived in 1971, a season after coach Vince Lombardi had died, he didn't come to carry out a longtime franchise tradition of losing. Allen promised "the future is now," then backed it up by trading for a number of veteran players. The over-the-hill gang included nine starters thirty years or older.

The Cowboys had won the NFC in 1970 before losing to Baltimore in Super Bowl V. A year later they won the NFC again, this time getting drilled by Miami in the Super Bowl. So if the Redskins were to do anything, they'd have to beat Dallas. They'd already snapped a six-game losing streak to Dallas in 1971. But the teams had split during the 1972 season, each winning at home.

Washington had exorcised one ghost a week earlier when it defeated Green Bay 16–3 for its first playoff win since 1943, setting up a third meeting in this intensifying rivalry on New Year's Eve. Allen told the players the week of the game that this was "the biggest game of their lives." He'd used that phrase before, but this time he meant it.

For the fans this game meant everything as well. Four years earlier racial riots rocked the city, and the Redskins would turn into a galvanizing force, uniting a city like no other team in town could. "The people were crazy," Talbert said. "You would go around the Beltway and someone would be leaning out the window with a piece of paper wanting an autograph, and you're going 60 to 70 miles per hour. Those people really are the greatest football fans in the country."

Those fans were about to be treated to a New Year's memory they'd never forget. They got that thanks in part to a number of the over-the-hill gang members, including Kilmer. When Allen traded for him, he assumed he would always be Sonny Jurgensen's backup. Few would have disagreed. But Allen liked what Kilmer had to offer, preferring his manage-the-game style to Jurgensen's penchant for big passing. Not that he had much choice in 1972 after Jurgensen tore his Achilles tendon in October.

Kilmer won but it wasn't always pretty; his ball fluttered to his targets compared to the artistry of Jurgensen's tight spirals. Jurgensen was a Redskins hero since they traded for him in 1964. Kilmer was a converted running back who once nearly had his foot amputated after a 1963 car accident. He started four years for New Orleans before arriving in Washington, igniting the most famous quarterback controversy in Redskins history. Fans used bumper stickers to show their allegiance, one proclaiming, "I Love Billy" and another reading, "I Love Sonny." Thing is, the quarterbacks became fast friends, remaining close to this day.

"Sonny and I hit it off right away," Kilmer said. "Instead of being petty, we decided to help each other. We knew there wasn't one healthy body between us, and neither of us could play the whole season."

This day would belong to Kilmer. Washington led 10–3 entering the final period, helped by Kilmer's 15-yard touchdown pass to Taylor in the second quarter, set up when the pair connected on a 51-yard pass, beating corner Charlie Waters.

A quiet third quarter left the game close going into the final fifteen minutes. That would change thirty-eight seconds into the fourth period. On third-and-10 from Dallas's 45 yard line, with Waters having been sidelined with a broken arm, Kilmer tested backup corner Mark Washington. Once again, Kilmer found Taylor for a long touchdown pass and 17–3 lead. He would finish with 14 completions in 18 attempts for 194 yards and 2 touchdowns, but this pass is the one most remembered. "I just told Charley to run as far as he could," Kilmer said. "I thought I had overthrown him. I don't know how he got it. It was an electrifying moment."

But the most electric moment came after Bob Brunet's jarring hit on a kickoff return following Curt Knight's second field goal of the quarter. "The stands were rocking," Redskins defensive tackle Bill Brundige said. "You could literally feel the sound cascading in your body. It was so incredible. Jack Pardee was calling signals in the huddle. I was about a foot and a half from him and he was yelling as loud as he could, and I couldn't hear a thing he said. When the Cowboys trotted to the line, you could see their heads turning left and right, and you could see it going through their minds, 'What in the hell am I doing here?'"

They needn't have worried; they were going home soon, 26–3 losers after Knight kicked yet another field goal. The fans didn't wait until midnight to celebrate, swarming the field as the final gun sounded. Redskins players lifted Allen onto their shoulders, carrying him off the field.

The Redskins had announced themselves as a true contender

## Learning Experience

Former trainer Bubba Tyer was the Redskins' biggest fan and sometimes one of its most intense ones, too. After a 20–16 win at Dallas in his first season in 1971, Tyer celebrated walking off the field.

"I was walking off the field with [assistant coach] Mike McCormack and [the Redskins tunnel] is on the left and the Cowboys were on the right," Tyer said, "and I'm all excited. We'd just beaten the Dallas Cowboys! I'm whooping and hollering, and Mike grabs me around the neck and says, 'Hey, we play them again in six weeks.' I thought, 'Welcome to the NFL.'"

to the rest of the NFL. They took a supposedly aging roster with a wobbly throwing quarterback and unseated a team that had grown accustomed to postseason success. "We were a bunch of guys who weren't supposed to be able to play," Taylor said. "But we fooled America."

Ten seasons later, the Redskins thumped Dallas again in the NFC title game, winning 31–17. The road to Super Bowl XVII started after a first-round playoff win against Detroit, the fans anticipating—craving—one matchup in particular.

"We want Dallas!"

Then it continued the following week. After the Redskins grabbed a 7–0 lead against Minnesota in a second-round playoff game, the fans let their wishes be known, ignoring the fact that the game against the Vikings was far from over.

"We want Dallas! We want Dallas!"

Call it the "chants" of a lifetime, for the crowd received what it wanted in the 1982 playoffs, drawing Dallas for the NFC Championship Game. And they maintained their fervor for those three words throughout the week. As Redskins staff drove to old Redskins Park, they saw banners expressing one sentiment: "We want Dallas!" At the Cowboys' hotel, fans gathered outside and shouted the new mantra some more.

"We got there and the stadium was half-full an hour before the game," said former Redskins general manager Charley Casserly. "You never saw that many people in pregame. When the Cowboys came out, the fans chanted, 'We want Dallas!' You were getting chills."

"They started rocking the place," Redskins tight end Rick "Doc" Walker said. "I was thinking, 'Dallas has to be superhuman to survive this.'"

Until that game, Washington hadn't produced many chills against Dallas, having lost six straight. The Redskins had not reached the playoffs since 1976 and had not advanced to the NFC Championship Game since the 1972 season.

Dallas had been part of the reason for the lack of success, particularly at the end of the 1979 season, when a 35–34 comeback victory cost Washington a playoff spot. The Redskins had changed coaches twice since their last playoff appearance, first going with Jack Pardee for three seasons, and then replacing him with Joe Gibbs in 1981.

Meanwhile, Dallas remained under Tom Landry's guidance. Since the 1976 season, the Cowboys had won a Super Bowl (XII in the 1977 season), lost another one (XIII), and lost in consecutive NFC championships (1980 and 1981). Topping it off, Dallas handed Washington its only loss during the nine-game, strike-shortened 1982 season.

So while Redskins fans chanted, "We Want Dallas!" others said, "Are you sure?" The players were sure.

"That day was the most intense I can remember ever seeing my teammates, to a man," Grant said. "There were comments made the week before the game by Dallas that they would prepare to go from Washington to Pasadena for the Super Bowl [played a week later]. There could not have been any greater motivational point than that."

The intensity trickled down to the coaching staff. Before the game, Redskins offensive line coach Joe Bugel did something he never did: chain-smoked. Then, after the national anthem, Bugel shouted across the field to Dallas defensive line coach Ernie Stautner—and flipped him the bird.

But all stories from this game return to the chant. Walker remembered running back John Riggins taking the field an hour and fifteen minutes before kickoff, just to jog. "And the diesel horn went off," Walker said. "That was chilling . . . But you still had to caution yourself not to get too caught up in that—you never do. [End] Dexter [Manley] was hyperventilating, and at that point you can't hear anything because the crowd is going nuts."

The Redskins built a 14–3 lead, scoring on a touchdown pass from Joe Theismann to Charlie Brown and later Riggins's touchdown run, set up by Monte Coleman's fumble recovery at Dallas's 11 yard line. Manley knocked Dallas quarterback Danny White from the game, giving him a concussion late in the first half. With backup Gary Hogeboom having thrown only 8 career passes, a rout appeared imminent. Those who thought that way were disappointed—and for a while, very nervous.

Hogeboom dented the lead with a 6-yard touchdown pass to Drew Pearson. Then, after Mike Nelms's 76-yard kickoff return set up a 4-yard touchdown run by Riggins, Hogeboom struck again. This time he connected with Butch Johnson for 23 yards, capping an 84-yard drive. With 3:25 left in the third quarter, Washington led only 21–17.

The Redskins caught a break when Rafael Septien missed a 42-yard field goal, a crucial miss considering Mark Moseley would kick a 29-yarder in the fourth quarter, set up by linebacker Mel Kaufman's interception.

A day of emotion would reach a crescendo one play later. On Dallas's first play from scrimmage following Moseley's field goal, Manley and Grant combined to put the game out of reach. On first down, Hogeboom wanted to throw a screen pass to Dorsett. Earlier in the game this play had gained 25 yards. This time it ended Dallas's hopes.

Grant read the screen and headed out to the flat. Meanwhile Manley bulled his way toward Hogeboom and tipped the ball. Grant intercepted at the 10 and high-stepped his way for a touchdown and 31–17 lead. Grant spiked the ball, a moment captured on the cover of *Sports Illustrated* the following week. "I hear about that play maybe every other day, if not every day," said Grant, who played in Washington through 1990 and still works in the area. "It's humbling. People constantly come up and tell you stories of relatives who saw that game, and they remember how happy they were. It's very heartwarming. I never realized the impact that would have on so many people. I'll be at a restaurant and someone buys me a meal. Other people said their relative was in the hospital and that was the last thing they saw. And I think I've met every single person who sat in the end zone that day."

When the Redskins got the ball back, they had one thought on their minds: Run out the clock. And they only had one play on their minds: 50-Gut, a Riggins run up the middle plowing through holes opened by the "Hogs" on the offensive line. They ran it nine straight times, even telling Dallas defensive tackle Randy White what was coming. It didn't matter.

And when the clock wound down, the noise level increased. "[The fans] were unbelievable," Dorsett said. "You could tell they were waiting for us and wanted us for a while, and they showed it. Their team delivered what they wanted. I wish that our fans

*Linebacker Jay Leeuwenberg (57) with Cowboys defensive lineman Alonzo Spellman in a December 2000 game. L. M. Otero/AP*

could be as boisterous as Redskins fans. Fans don't realize what that does for a team to have that kind of support."

"I was scared, I was elated, I was overwhelmed," Theismann said. "People can't appreciate this, but it was the only time I actually felt the ground shake beneath my feet in that stadium. The fans were pounding away on those metal stands with such force and in such great unison that as I stood on the field and the clock wound down . . . I'm an emotional person anyway, and my emotions overwhelmed me. Tears came to my eyes and the ground was shaking. I thought, 'This is beyond belief. These were a bunch of guys no one gave any credit to and now we're about to beat the vaunted Dallas Cowboys.' We were going to the Super Bowl."

# The Quarterback Club

The joke around Washington is this: The only person more popular than the president is the quarterback of the Redskins. Actually, it might not be such a joke. "Presidents come see us play," former Redskins quarterback Joe Theismann said. "I'm not paying seventy dollars to sit in the White House and watch them work. This franchise is very storied when it comes to quarterbacks. From Sammy Baugh to Eddie LeBaron to Sonny

Jurgensen and the toughness of Billy Kilmer, the era I had, the great game Doug Williams had, and the season Mark Rypien had." But three stand out: Baugh, Jurgensen, and Theismann.

## Sammy Baugh

Maybe all one needs to know about Sammy Baugh is that a few years ago, some of the most respected NFL writers gathered to hold a mock draft, selecting from a pool of every former player. Baugh was the first pick.

Those selecting knew that Baugh could win games passing, punting, or intercepting passes. But perhaps nothing showed his impact more than one day in the early 1990s, when Sonny Jurgensen, himself a Redskins legend and fellow Hall of Famer, showed up in Texas for an interview, a little wowed by his host.

They talked about defenses and how they reacted to certain situations and receivers. As Baugh did this, Jurgensen watched with pleasure as the eighty-something ex-quarterback became more animated, spitting tobacco into a tin coffee can. He'd demonstrate this pass or another pass. He also happened to, um, urinate in the bathroom while still miked, providing a few chuckles for the camera crew. Then there was the cussing. In the three-hour taped interview, many of the stories weren't usable because they were laced with salty language. "That was one of the most enjoyable days I spent," Jurgensen said. "It was so much fun, just to talk to him about the game. He told me things I couldn't believe."

In many ways, it's hard to believe what Baugh accomplished, given how much the game has changed. But in his day, most of the top players had to play both ways because of the small rosters.

So in 1943, Baugh led the NFL in passing—and he led the league with eleven interceptions while playing defense. He also led the NFL in punting that season.

The career numbers are impressive: He's either first or second on the NFL's all-time passing list in nine different categories, including most seasons leading the league (he shares the mark of six with Steve Young). He also intercepted 31 passes in his career and still holds the NFL record for punting average in a season at 51.4 yards. It's no wonder he was among the inaugural class in the Pro Football Hall of Fame, as well as a member of the NFL's 75th Anniversary All-Time team.

The fact that three other quarterbacks shared the stage on the all-time team irked longtime *Washington Post* sportswriter Shirley Povich, who wrote in 1994: "Sammy Baugh deserves far better than a quarter of a loaf. No disrespect to Johnny Unitas and Joe Montana and Otto Graham . . . They lacked his measure in so many skills."

Baugh also served as the centerpiece for owner George Preston Marshall's sales pitch. He sold Baugh as a real ol' cowboy, a true Western hero. Baugh even showed up in Washington dressed in a Stetson cowboy hat and boots, living up to his image. Except, as he has told numerous people, "Those were the first boots I ever had. They were killing my feet."

Baugh wasn't a regular cowboy, though he has spent most of his life on a 7,500-acre farm in Rotan, Texas, and eventually performed in some rodeos. The only time he lived elsewhere was when he played, and later coached, football. Even then he'd return there in the off-season with his family.

That was home, and Texas is where Baugh learned to throw the ball. He'd hang a tire by a rope from a tree limb. Then he'd swing the tire back and forth, throwing balls through the opening

Quarterback Sammy Baugh (33) drops back to pass against the Chicago Bears in 1942. AP

from 10 to 20 yards away, sometimes on the run. After doing this for hours, Baugh became incredibly accurate, leading to another oft-told tale. In his first practice with Washington, coach Ray Flaherty told Baugh he wanted him to hit receiver Wayne Millner in the eye. "Which eye?" Baugh supposedly replied.

Baseball also held a soft spot in Baugh's heart—he received his nickname of Slingin' Sammy from his play at third base for Texas Christian University. And Baugh played minor league baseball in the St. Louis Cardinals organization for three seasons (he was signed by then-scout Rogers Hornsby). He might have stuck with it, too, but he recognized that he'd have a tough time winning a job in the major leagues. Besides, he said, "I couldn't hit the curve very well."

But he could throw. Baugh perfected the art of throwing from all angles, completing passes underhanded, from his ear, sidearm, and off-balance. He also favored the short pass, owing to his days at TCU under coach Dutch Meyer.

And he knew to unload the ball quick. After he was switched from tailback in the Single Wing to quarterback in the T-formation in 1944, Baugh had the center snap the ball toward his right ear, putting him in position for a faster pass. He also eventually made the Redskins' offense unpredictable, with his then-unheard-of penchant for throwing on first or second down. Early in Baugh's career, it was a penalty if a player on the field talked to someone on the sidelines, leaving the play-calling to the quarterback.

The T-formation prolonged his career, with Baugh once saying, "I hated the T when we went to it in 1944, but my body loved it. I probably would have lasted a year or two more as a Single Wing tailback, my body was so beat up. But the T gave me nine more seasons."

Redskins fans were thankful for that. In 1947, they even honored him when the Touchdown Club gave him a station wagon in a pregame ceremony. Baugh responded with one of his greatest efforts, throwing 6 touchdown passes in a rainy-day, 45–21 win over the Chicago Cardinals. The Cardinals would go on to win the Eastern Division; Washington would finish 4–8.

In a 1943 game against Detroit, Baugh threw 4 touchdown passes and intercepted 4 passes, setting a record he now shares with seventeen others. Not that it impressed Baugh "You've got to remember, in our day you could not throw the ball away under a rush," he told Jurgensen. "You had to throw it at a receiver. And

I had Dick Todd on one side and Andy Farkas on another. Where are you gonna throw? You throw at me so I get all the balls."

Call it modesty because those who watched him play never doubted his ability on either side of the ball, though he stopped playing defense after 1943. But he made his name on offense, setting a path for future quarterbacks to follow. Some say none have surpassed him. Povich, who saw the other greats play, once summed up a column on Baugh this way: "No other QB can claim his fame."

## Sonny Jurgensen

There's no need for a last name and there hasn't been for years. His first name, Sonny, conjures up images: a round-bellied quarterback throwing the tightest spirals around the field, leading the Redskins to big scoring days; an older man chomping on cigars, growing frustrated by the latest lack of success yet picking them to win each week.

Sonny Jurgensen came to Washington via an April Fool's Day trade, but his association with the club has been anything but a joke. Perhaps nobody has been a greater Redskins ambassador than Jurgensen, thanks to his television and radio work over the years. Jurgensen has been associated with the Redskins since 1964. That means enduring endless autograph and interview requests. "It's just something that's been a part of my life as long as I can remember," Jurgensen said. "When I was playing, I was very close to the fans, and that's one of the reasons I think I was accepted. We didn't have great teams by any means. But we did the best we could, and people appreciated that."

Jurgensen made the Pro Bowl four times in his first six

# Uniformity

**The best quarterbacks in franchise history had one thing in common: They were the only players to wear their respective jersey numbers. Sammy Baugh (33), Sonny Jurgensen (9), and Joe Theismann (7) all remain the only players to wear those particular numbers. Baugh's is the only officially retired number.**

seasons in Washington. He still owns or shares four Redskins passing records, and he captured three NFL passing titles. Not that it led to success: During his first six seasons, Washington finished with a winning record only once. However, they owned one of the game's most feared offenses. His 1983 induction into the Hall of Fame was a no-brainer. But his appeal went beyond pure statistics. It went to his belly. "People looked at me and said, 'Damn, if he can do it, then I can sit here, have my beer, and go out,'" Jurgensen said. "But I just had a bad tailor, my uniform was cut badly."

Pause for laughter. Now continue.

"But I'd get my arm in great condition," he said. "We'd go out and throw and I did very little running. That wasn't something I was paid to do. My thing was, don't judge me on what I look like; judge me on how I play."

Vince Lombardi once called him the "best he's ever seen." And former Redskins defensive coordinator Richie Petitbon, a defensive back in the 1960s and 1970s, said, "Had Sonny played with a defense, he would have won more championships than anybody."

Of course, some of his fan appeal went to his fun-loving ways. Few enjoyed the nightlife like Jurgensen did, and his stories became legendary. Once he even dragged a coach's son into the mix. As Jurgensen snuck out after curfew in training camp in Carlisle, he happened upon Dewey Graham sitting on the curb outside. So he brought him along. While they were out, Jurgensen learned that the coaches had performed a double bed check. He was busted.

So when he returned, rather than wait to be fined, he knocked on coach Otto Graham's door. "Otto came to the door in his pajamas and said, 'What are you waking me up for?' I said, 'I was out and didn't want to be fined a lot of money, so I'm supposed to let you know when I get back in,'" said Jurgensen. "He starts screaming at me and said, 'Who were you out with?' I said, 'him.'" That's when Graham noticed his son. "He kicked him out of camp," Jurgensen said.

But Jurgensen performed during this time, even in pain. After the 1967 season a doctor, after performing surgery on his elbow, told Jurgensen to consider another profession, telling the quarterback of calcium deposits that had eroded the muscle. Jurgensen pleaded with him not to tell anyone else. Then he went out and threw 5 touchdown passes in the 1968 season opener against Chicago.

Not all was smooth for Jurgensen in Washington, particularly under coach George Allen, who arrived in 1971. Their relationship was rough from the start, from the time when the Allens were looking to buy a house. Before they had found one, they visited Jurgensen at home. "Their driver told me later on," Jurgensen said, "that when they came to my house—it was an old Mediterranean place—and walked up, Allen's wife, Ettie, said,

'This is what I want. We can have this if you trade him.'"

Jurgensen had enjoyed playing for the offensive-minded Vince Lombardi only two years earlier. That season, he completed 62 percent of his passes and threw 22 touchdown passes against 15 interceptions. Lombardi told others that if he'd had Jurgensen in Green Bay, he never would have lost. Allen, though, was a coach who relied on special teams and defense.

Jurgensen enjoyed needling Allen. He'd sometimes ignore the play call (usually a run), opting for something more aggressive (a pass). When Billy Kilmer was starting ahead of him, Jurgensen would tweak Allen in practice. "I would run the two-minute drill for the opponent," Jurgensen said. "There was one pass they could not stop, and I'd throw it and he'd get upset. Once he said, 'Throw an incompletion and let's kick a field goal.' And I threw a touchdown pass. It just burned him up. But that was my arrogance, my stubbornness."

When the Redskins reached the Super Bowl in the 1972 season, an injured Jurgensen wasn't allowed to stand on the sidelines. Instead, they put him in a booth by himself, perhaps the lowest point of Jurgensen's career. It warmed him when Miami coach Don Shula greeted him on the field before the game, telling him, "It would be a better game if you were here."

During the game Jurgensen watched Kilmer struggle with the Dolphins' two-deep zone in the 14–7 loss. "I always felt we would have won if I had the opportunity to play," Jurgensen said, "or if they had just let me talk to Billy. Years after that, [former assistant coach Joe Sullivan] told me that Allen felt I might be a distraction, and that was the reason they put me up there."

Two years later, the Redskins hosted the Dolphins. Allen decided to start the forty-year-old Jurgensen, looking for a spark.

"He said to me, 'A lot of coaches wouldn't start a forty-year-old quarterback,'" Jurgensen said. "I said, 'You will if you want to win.'" And the Redskins did win, with Jurgensen leading a last-minute drive in a 20–17 victory. That was his last hurrah as Jurgensen retired following the season. He embarked on a commentating career, winding up in the Redskins radio broadcast booth. Fans grew to love his personality in the booth, especially when paired with former teammate Sam Huff.

Nowadays it's still hard for Jurgensen to eat an uninterrupted meal in Washington—or in other cities sometimes. The night before a 2004 game at Pittsburgh, as Jurgensen sat in a restaurant, ten Redskins fans who had grown up in Alexandria, Virginia, approached the old redhead, telling him, "Hey! We watched you all the time!"

It's funny how life works out: Jurgensen was a Pro Bowl passer for Philadelphia, setting a club record with 32 scoring tosses in 1961. Then one day, an hour or so after meeting with Philadelphia's coach, Joe Kuharich, Jurgensen was traded to Washington on a day reserved for practical jokes. "I was shocked," Jurgensen said. "But in the long run, it was the best thing that happened to me."

## Joe Theismann

This will come as no surprise; not to any Redskins fan. Not to any former teammate of Joe's. Not to anyone who has watched him analyze games on ESPN. "I would be lying to you if I said I didn't love center stage," Joe Theismann said.

And the stage loved him back, for in his twelve-year Redskins career, few players provided more entertainment for the organization than Theismann did, whether it was dramatic plays or gruesome injuries or leading the franchise to its first Super Bowl. He snuck onto the field for punt returns. He played in one game despite having two teeth knocked out. He became the NFL's MVP, leading the offense to a record year. Dallas fans hated him, taunting him after a 44–14 win in 1985 by singing "Happy Birthday," hardly the desired gift.

Redskins quarterbacks Sonny Jurgensen and Billy Kilmer weren't fond of him, either. Theismann arrived in 1974, obtained in a trade with Miami, which drafted him in the fourth round out of Notre Dame three years earlier. But Theismann didn't want to sit behind Bob Griese and instead played the next three seasons in Canada. He didn't like to sit behind anybody.

When Theismann arrived in Washington, he told reporters that he went there to be a starter, which Jurgensen and Kilmer later translated into, "I'm going to put those two old men on the bench."

"Billy and Sonny united against the common enemy," Theismann said. "I know that. I think that situation made me a tougher, smarter player. Part of being a quarterback in any city is public relations as well. At times you can be candid and frank. Other times you have to be politically correct." Theismann later said he regretted even saying what he did.

"I think the world of Billy as a player," he said. "No one was tougher. He could get guys to play at a level for him that other quarterbacks would dream about. Sonny was the best pure passer ever to put on a uniform. I used to stand in practice in awe of the way he threw it. When you're young and in competition, you get mad and angry at people. I wanted something they had. They were proud men, and they didn't want to give it up. Hence, you get yourself a conflict."

Theismann didn't become the full-time starter until 1978,

*Joe Theismann celebrates after completing a touchdown pass in Super Bowl XVII.* AP

holding the job until his infamous leg injury on November 18, 1985. That was the longest uninterrupted stretch by a Redskins starting quarterback since Sammy Baugh's fifteen-year stint (1937 to 1951).

But Theismann's first action came as a punt returner in a 1974 game against the Giants. Washington's top returner, Herb Mul-Key, was hurt. His backup, safety Kenny Houston, got banged up and had to leave the game. Theismann took advantage. He had fielded punts in practice so, with Houston hurting, Theismann ran up to coach George Allen and said, "Do you want me to return punts?" Without looking, Allen said yes.

When Theismann ran onto the field, Allen shouted, "What's he doing out there?" Coaches yelled at Theismann to return. "But once I stepped onto the field, I wasn't turning around," he said. Theismann returned 15 punts that season.

"If I could go back and play one more game, I would return punts before playing quarterback," Theismann said. "It's the biggest rush in the world. I still laugh when I watch a punt return I had against the Rams, a 42-yarder. I remember the Super Bowls, but I also remember on a return in Dallas I broke through the line and had a shot to go to the end zone, but someone just caught my heel. I looked up and all I saw was open field."

But Theismann was so much more than just a confident player who returned punts. He's also the Redskins' career leader in passing yards (25,206), attempts (3,602), and completions (2,044). In 1983, one season after leading the Redskins to a Super Bowl victory, Theismann earned NFL MVP honors. When Joe Gibbs came to Washington in 1981, he and Theismann had a long talk about what they needed from each other after the team

# Bad Break

The most gruesome injury in Redskins history occurred on November 18, 1985, when New York Giants linebacker Lawrence Taylor sacked Joe Theismann from behind, breaking his leg. No one knew it that night, but it turned out to be a career-ending injury.

"They put me on a stretcher," Theismann said, "and I turned to [New York's] Harry Carson and said, 'Harry, I understand you're thinking about retiring.' He said, 'Yes, I am.' I said, 'Well, don't you go retiring because I'm coming back.' And he said, 'That may be the case, pal, but it ain't gonna be tonight.'" Theismann never did make it back to the playing field.

started 0–5. "I had a lot of things going for me before Joe got here," Theismann said. "I had radio and TV shows, and I don't think he was convinced that I was committed to football the way that he was or the way he wanted his quarterback to be. When we came to an understanding, that's when this team took off."

Gibbs said, "Joe was highly motivated and had a burning desire to be a great player. He'd taken some criticism and abuse, and he wanted to show people. You could see that in the way he practiced and played. The thing I remember the most about him was not the Super Bowls, it was that Giants game."

No, not the one that ended his career in 1985 on a Monday night. Gibbs was referring to the game in 1982 when Theismann threw 4 first-half interceptions on a snowy day at RFK Stadium. In that game, Theismann, who never wore a mouthpiece, had his two front teeth knocked out, courtesy of New York's Byron Hunt. His helmet got inside Theismann's one-bar face mask. "I spit out my teeth, went to the sideline, and talked to Joe for a second," Theismann said. "I convinced him I could still talk. I had a lisp. It was easy to say 'Hut.' Joe said he was going to take me out and I said, 'No, you're not.' I didn't break a nerve, but it was close. So I had to be careful when I took a deep breath. Anyone with a cavity in their mouth can appreciate when the cold air hits."

More than twenty years later, Gibbs said he remembers exactly what he was thinking as Theismann led the Redskins back from a 14–3 deficit for a 15–14 victory. "This man is a tough dude."

And that's all Theismann wanted to hear. "If someone asked how I'd like to be remembered," he said, "I would hope that my teammates and 'Skins fans would say first, that he's a really tough guy, and second, that he did everything he could to help the team win."

# The Roaring Sixties

The Redskins entered the 1960s as one of the worst teams in football. They exited the decade as merely mediocre. In between, they were both, creating an almost exact duplicate of the previous decade. Unlike the 1950s, however, this decade proved to be memorable. They went through three coaches, but one happened to be a Hall of Fame quarterback and the other was regarded as possibly the best coach of all time. They also played in a new stadium that would become legendary. And they acquired their first African-American player and developed a feared passing attack.

Five players who spent at least four seasons in Washington during the 1960s eventually reached the Pro Football Hall of Fame: quarterback Sonny Jurgensen, running back Bobby Mitchell, receiver Charley Taylor, linebacker Sam Huff, and safety Paul Krause. That's four more players than have made it to Canton from the Super Bowl teams of the 1980s and 1991. And during this decade, the Redskins started a string of home sellouts that hasn't ended. They never won more than seven games, but the games were interesting.

## A New Home

When it opened, some fans said it was better than the new stadium built in Rome for the Olympic Games. Others weren't as impressed, upset that nearly 400 seats still hadn't been installed before the first game, and a few women complained that the bathrooms lacked privacy and mirrors and were "worse than in Paris." Yet when the $24 million stadium opened in October of 1961, it was considered state of the art. It was also needed, as old Griffith Stadium had become too small, seating fewer than 31,000 fans. Despite the Redskins' lack of recent success, their fan base was growing. And D.C. Stadium, which could seat as many as 55,000, was just right.

The new stadium would house baseball's Washington Senators, not to mention the Beatles, the Rolling Stones, and, eventually, the Olympics and World Cup soccer games, too. However, it was the Redskins who made it famous.

The stadium also forced Washington to finally integrate.

# Home Games

The Redskins enjoyed playing at RFK Stadium, their home from 1961 to 1996. Washington went 173-102-3 at RFK, including 11-1 in the playoffs. The franchise moved into its current home, FedEx Field, in 1997. Washington won its first regular-season game there in dramatic fashion, beating Arizona 19-13 in overtime. After the Cardinals' Kevin Butler tied the score at 13-13 with two seconds remaining in regulation, the Redskins won it on Gus Frerotte's 40-yard touchdown pass to Michael Westbrook 1:36 into overtime.

Secretary of the Interior Stewart Udall told Redskins owner George Preston Marshall the team would be evicted if it didn't integrate (becoming the last NFL team to do so). Because the stadium was built on federal land, Marshall had to comply. By the end of the 1961 season, Washington would trade for future Hall of Famer Bobby Mitchell.

The first game wasn't memorable. The New York Giants defeated Washington 24-21 before 36,767 fans, at the time the largest sports gathering in the city's history. The Redskins' first victory in the stadium came that December, when running back Dick James set a club record that still stands by scoring 4 touchdowns in a 34-24 win over Dallas. Eight years later, the building was renamed RFK Stadium, honoring Robert F. Kennedy.

Whatever the name, fans there witnessed some of the greatest moments in Redskins history. Amazingly, the Redskins started selling out in 1966 despite a wretched previous twenty seasons (which included only three winning years). That string hasn't ended. Washington won two NFC Championship Games in the stadium, both over Dallas. The Redskins created a massive home-field advantage in the 1970s and 1980s with a combination of talented teams and enthusiastic fans. Big plays in big games would leave the stadium shaking, particularly the portable lower stands. The stadium remains, but the Redskins left after the 1996 season.

"It was the little things," former Redskins quarterback Joe Theismann said, "like the locker room. Our lockers at old Redskins Park were nicer. There had to be a hundred layers of paint on those lockers at RFK. And it was the way the wind blew in that stadium, and the fact that we never had grass. We mostly played on painted dirt. The great thing about a stadium like that is the memories will live on forever."

Former Redskins safety Ken Houston made the most memorable tackle there, a goal-line stop of Dallas's Walt Garrison to preserve a 14–7 win in 1973. That's not his favorite memory, though. "I remember we're playing Philadelphia," he said, "and it was snowing. I have a picture from this game of George Allen on the sideline talking to Billy Kilmer, and the snow is falling. I love that picture. Something about that stadium was special, especially in the winter when they'd turn the lights on. My greatest memory of RFK was RFK itself."

# April 1964

Eagles quarterback Sonny Jurgensen left a meeting with his coach on April Fool's Day, convinced his next year in Philadelphia would be better. Less than an hour later, Jurgensen, sitting in a Philadelphia deli, found out even more about his next season: It would be spent in Washington. Eight days later, New York Giants linebacker Sam Huff received a call at a former teammate's bar in Cleveland that floored him with similar news: He, too, had been traded to the Redskins.

In a short span, the Redskins forever changed the face of their franchise. They gave up quarterback Norm Snead and defensive back Claude Crabb to get Jurgensen; they traded popular running back Dick James and defensive tackle Andy Stynchula to land Huff. But they received two players who still haven't left. Jurgensen and Huff roomed together, became close friends, and, in 1981, first were paired on Redskins broadcasts, where they've been ever since. Huff said he "couldn't have a better friend than Sonny."

Jurgensen, a quarterback, quickly accepted this move in 1964. He liked Redskins coach Bill McPeak, his family and friends in North Carolina could now follow him closer, and he could have a fresh start away from the boo-birds of Philadelphia.

Huff, a linebacker, didn't feel the same way. Even now the trade that ended his glorious eight-year run with the Giants bothers him. Jurgensen had started for only three seasons in Philadelphia, a stretch that included little success. He played eleven seasons in Washington, making four Pro Bowls and finishing as one of the most beloved players in franchise history. Meanwhile, Huff was the face of the Giants defense. He helped lead New York to six NFL Championship Games, winning once, and was the focus of a CBS documentary called *The Violent World of Sam Huff*. News of his trade even ran across the Wall Street ticker tape. The media swarmed his house in New York, awaiting his arrival. And Huff knew this: New York had dominated Washington, posting a 13–2–1 record against the Redskins in his eight seasons. Overall, Washington was 13–48–5 in the five years before Huff arrived, hardly a tempting organization for anyone to join.

After the trade, Huff called Cleveland owner Art Modell, a former New Yorker who used to hang around the Giants before buying the Browns. "I wanted to see if he would trade for me," Huff said. "I would liked to have played for the Browns. I knew the Browns well, and they seemed to be a good organization. I didn't know anyone with the Redskins. But Modell said he couldn't stop it. He said, 'Go to Washington. You're a great player, you'll make it work.'"

So that's what Huff did. He played five seasons for the Redskins—only one of which ended with a winning record—and served as an assistant coach for one more. Though his best days were in New York, he's also on the Redskins 70 Greatest Players list. He's on a similar list for New York. He's also in the Pro Football Hall of Fame.

Huff, who started broadcasting Redskins games in 1974, laughs when asked how long it took him to get over the trade, saying, "Probably a lifetime . . . I'm torn even to this day."

When the Redskins play in New York, Huff is often asked to do radio or television shows. The TV studios will have big pictures of him around the set—in a Giants uniform, of course. And when some former players celebrated owner Wellington Mara's eightieth birthday in 1996, Huff was invited. "The treatment I get is like I never left," Huff said. "It's very difficult for me when I go back. You have so much success; you're playing in Yankee Stadium. It was a great time in sports. I have a hard time talking about it now. Linebackers never forgive and forget. Maybe you push it aside, but that's the way we're made. This is an emotional game. You can't play it unless you have emotion."

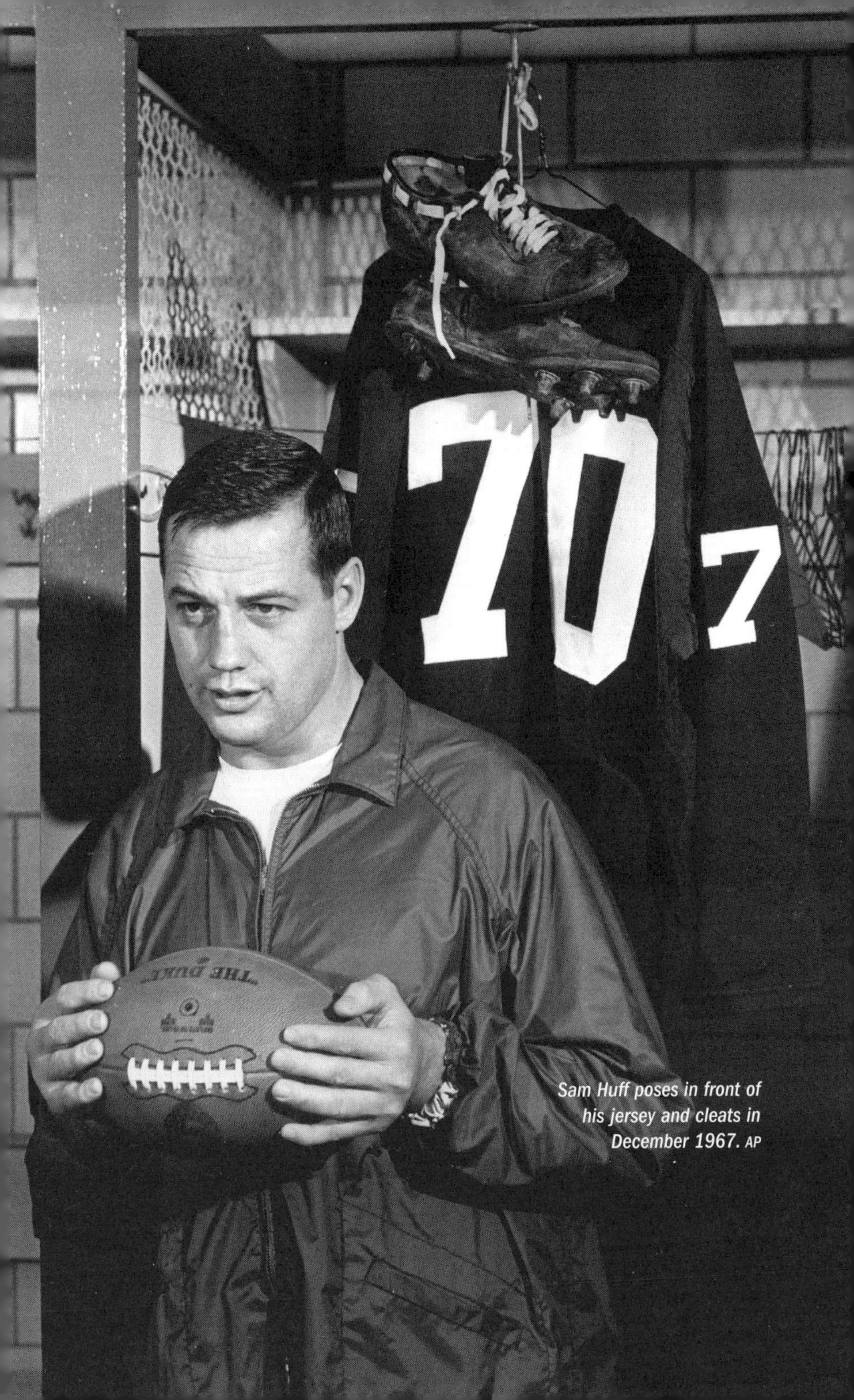


Sam Huff poses in front of his jersey and cleats in December 1967. AP

# The Greatest Comeback

They chanted for a guy who would soon fade into obscurity, preferring him to the already beloved passer, the one on a Hall of Fame path. Sonny Jurgensen couldn't blame the fans; the offense had produced zero points midway through the second quarter in this November 28, 1965, matchup. Meanwhile Dallas had raced to a 21–0 lead, further upsetting Redskins fans already angered over another season of futility. That marked twenty seasons and counting.

But their solution was odd: Bench Jurgensen for Dick Shiner? Washington already had tried that earlier in the season, and the results were predictable. After the Redskins produced only 24 points in their first three games, coach Bill McPeak started Shiner against St. Louis, only to watch the Redskins lose 37–16. Jurgensen remembered the coaches telling him to go into the game late. So he told them, "What do you think, that I have a 38-point play in my pocket? You made your bed, hey, good luck. Now you're seeing it wasn't me."

No, it wasn't. And this game against Dallas proved that Jurgensen remained a feared passer. Besides, the Redskins had won four of five before this matchup—after losing five straight to open the season.

The hot stretch didn't matter early against Dallas, as the Cowboys built their big second-quarter lead on a host of Redskins mistakes. Jurgensen threw interceptions on two of his first four passes. Star running back Charley Taylor lost a fumble early. Chants for Shiner, a star from the University of Maryland, started. "They did that a lot in those days," Jurgensen said.

"It was a bad day for everybody," Taylor said.

But Jurgensen and Taylor connected on a 26-yard scoring

pass before halftime. The extra point was blocked, but the Redskins sensed new life. That is, until Taylor fumbled again in the second half, leading to a Dallas field goal and 24–6 lead.

Still, the rally continued. Jurgensen snuck in from the 1 yard line capping a 90-yard drive, and running back Danny Lewis scored from the 2 yard line in the fourth quarter. Suddenly it was 24–20. Just as suddenly Dallas scored again for an 11-point lead with under six minutes remaining.

Three Jurgensen passes later, the final one a 10-yarder to receiver Bobby Mitchell, it was 31–27 with 3:32 to go. A 56-yard kickoff return set up Dallas at the Redskins 41 yard line, but Washington's defense eventually forced kicker Danny Villanueva to attempt a 45-yard field goal. He missed, his second failed attempt of the day. With 1:41 left, the Redskins were 80 yards from punctuating this rally. Turns out they didn't need that much time.

In thirty-seven seconds, the Redskins drove for the winning score. Perhaps no play was more impressive than Mitchell's 35-yard grab at the 5 yard line, bending over to catch a ball at his knees. On the next play, receiver Angelo Coia split wide, ran toward the end as if he were going to block him, then turned back out and caught the winning pass. One problem: 1:04 remained, giving Dallas a final opportunity. The Cowboys moved to the Redskins' 34, and on fourth down, they attempted a 44-yard field goal. But Lonnie Sanders, Washington's 6'3" defensive back, went through an alley created by Huff and Fred Williams and blocked the kick. The Redskins won 34–31.

A day that started with boos and chants for Shiner, who would last one more season in Washington, ended in a stirring comeback led by Jurgensen. Afterward, Jurgensen sarcastically told reporters, "I'm glad the crowd let me stay in. It was decent of them."

# Huff's Revenge

A player who had made five Pro Bowls, won an NFL championship and played in five others, and earned a spot in the Pro
Football Hall of Fame would call a lopsided win over a bad team
one of the best moments of his life. But for Huff, it was more than
a win. It was personal. And Washington's 72–41 record-setting
victory over the New York Giants in 1966 meant more to the
former Giants star than to anyone else on the Redskins roster.

The teams broke three NFL records, including most points
by one team, most points by both teams, and most combined
touchdowns (16); tied three more with most touchdowns by one
team (10 by the Redskins); had most combined extra points (14);
and had most extra points by one team (9 by the Redskins). Also,
officials lost sixteen balls in the stands.

The Redskins were an explosive group, led by quarterback
Sonny Jurgensen, receivers Charley Taylor and Bobby Mitchell,
and tight end Jerry Smith. By season's end, the latter three would
rank among the top ten in the league in receptions.

They entered this game having lost three straight, leaving
them with a 5–6 record. But New York was worse, owning a
1–8–1 record and one of the league's worst defenses. That's what
pleased Huff, who was still angry with coach Allie Sherman who
had traded him two years earlier. Huff never blamed the Giants
for the move, only Sherman, whom he felt gutted a championship defense with that trade and several others.

"I told Sonny, 'This is going to be the day,'" Huff said. "We're
out warming up and [coach] Otto Graham comes by and says to
me, 'What do you think today?' I said, 'Otto, let me tell you something. You show no mercy today. We're going to score a lot of

points.' He said he'd be happy if we won by 1 or 2 points. I said, 'Otto, we're going to beat the hell out of them. They have no defense. I'm telling you, lay it on them.'" Which is what the Redskins did. Thing is, New York earned its only win of the season in a 13–10 win over Washington a month earlier.

This game was different. Jurgensen threw 3 touchdown passes, including 2 to Taylor. Running back A. D. Whitfield scored 3 first-half touchdowns, 2 on runs. And safety Brig Owens returned a fumble and an interception for touchdowns. The climax, though, came with seven seconds left and Washington leading, 69–41. That's when Huff called time-out and shouted for the field-goal team, unbeknownst to Graham. By the time he knew, it was too late. Kicker Charlie Gogolak booted a 29-yard field goal for the final points.

"I didn't get close to Sherman because I would have hurt him if I could," Huff said nearly forty years later. "But I looked across the field and shouted, 'Justice is done, you SOB!' I hate to say it, but it was the greatest moment of my life because I got even."

## Vince Lombardi

He developed his reputation in Green Bay, where streets are named for him and his legend casts a long shadow. The guy with the gap-toothed grin and black glasses dominated the culture, earning the nickname St. Vince.

Vince Lombardi had no streets named for him in Washington. Nor did he dominate the NFL. But he did something equally remarkable: He ended the culture of losing in Washington. And that was no minor miracle.

*Vince Lombardi, head coach of the Washington Redskins, in 1970.* AP

The Redskins had endured thirteen straight seasons without a winning record. And they finished .500 only twice during that stretch. Nothing they tried worked until Lombardi came to Washington, a move that stunned the NFL. But Lombardi had resigned from the Packers coaching job in February of 1968 and become their general manager. That didn't satisfy his competitive drive, so he looked elsewhere. When the Redskins fired Graham following the 1968 season, their pursuit of Lombardi began. It turned out to be a wise move. Lombardi led Washington to a

7–5–2 record in 1969, clinching a winning mark with a 17–14 victory over New Orleans at RFK Stadium in week thirteen. "He changed what we'd been through before," Redskins linebacker Chris Hanburger said.

As in Green Bay, Lombardi demanded every ounce of a player's energy during practices and games. He tolerated nothing less from anyone. And heaven help the player who arrived late at his meetings, as the Redskins quickly learned. Lombardi had just finished introducing himself and his assistants to the players when fullback Ray McDonald, a first-round pick in 1967 and a starter that season and in 1968, arrived. "Lombardi went ballistic and shouted, 'Who are you?'" Redskins cornerback Pat Fischer recalled. "He cut him right there. Do you think anyone was ever late for a meeting after that? No one wanted to receive the wrath of Lombardi."

Lombardi also told the players his belief on conditioning. His theory: More games were won or lost in the final two minutes of each half. That meant his team must be in better shape than anyone else's. It sounded good, except to aging veterans like Huff, who weren't sure if they wanted to keep playing and who knew Lombardi from his early years as an assistant in New York. "I was afraid I couldn't make a training camp of his," Huff said. "When he said no one will out-condition our team, I thought, 'Oh no, here we go.'"

The old saying about Lombardi from his Packers players was humorous but true, as the Redskins soon found out: He treated everyone the same, like dogs. "There was no double standard," said Redskins running back Larry Brown, a rookie in 1969. "I liked him. I thought he was the toughest coach I ever worked for. But he made me a better player."

## Scared Straight

Head coach Vince Lombardi instilled a sense of fear, leaving no doubt who was in charge. At training camp in 1969, Lombardi told his players that when they went from the practice field to the main field at Dickinson College, they should go around the fields. So that's what linebacker Chris Hanburger was doing one day.

"Vince was riding his cart around and pulled up to me," Hanburger said. "He called you mister, probably because he didn't know our names. He said, 'Mister, how come you're not jogging around the field?' I said, 'In the meeting, you said we had to go around the fields, you didn't say how.' He shook his head back and forth and said, 'My God, have I mellowed.' Then I said, 'If you want me to jog, I'll jog.' From that point on, I jogged."

After nice-guy Graham, the Redskins needed a dose of discipline—at least some did. Jurgensen loved every minute of his time with Lombardi. Notorious for being out of shape, Jurgensen reported in the best shape of his life. But Lombardi never pestered Jurgensen about his weight. He knew that if he didn't report in shape, his training camp would get him there.

"I loved talking football with him," said Jurgensen, who responded by completing 62 percent of his passes and earning a Pro Bowl berth. "It was easy to see why Green Bay was so successful under him. He simplified the game and made it fun to play. In his schemes you didn't force balls, and if you did, it was a mental mistake. It was simply the best passing offense I ever played in."

Lombardi would convince the players that a play called 21 Quick Cut, a precursor to Joe Gibbs's 50 Gut, would be their best one. "He'd say, 'If we call this play, no one can stop us,'" Huff said. "He made you believe. That's what the great ones do."

But not everyone was pleased with Lombardi. Redskins center Len Hauss, a Pro Bowl player from 1967 to 1972, didn't like Lombardi's accusations. "That was the most miserable year of my life in football," Hauss said. "If you're giving 110 percent and working as hard as you can, you don't appreciate being called a dog and a quitter and worthless. I never quit a day in my life. Sonny's favorite line was, 'Boy, this is great. Lombardi kicks us in the ass and makes us give 100 percent.' I said, 'Yeah, Sonny, you have to be kicked in the ass to give 100 percent. I don't.'

"Vince and I had a volatile relationship. On the plane after the last game he came up to me, grabbed me, flashed that grin, and said, 'Let me tell you something, it's going to be better next year. You're going to enjoy it and you're not going to be pissed off the whole year.'" But next year didn't come for Lombardi. Feeling ill the following summer, he was initially diagnosed with a stomach virus. But exploratory surgery on June 27 revealed that he had a benign tumor in his colon. Exactly one month later, more surgery reversed that diagnosis; the tumor was malignant.

Lombardi died on September 3, 1970. Interim coach Bill Austin couldn't keep the Redskins headed down the same path Lombardi was leading them as they finished 6–8. But the 1969 season ranked as the club's best in fourteen years. Even Hauss knew what had happened. "His attitude was contagious among players and coaches and the fans," Hauss said. "You name it. He turned it around. He started changing the mind-set of not only the team, but also the fans."

# Hog Wild

In 1983 Columbia University alumni honored former Redskins tackle George Starke, along with three others, for distinguished professional achievement. Starke spent four days researching and writing his speech, only to ditch the opening at the last minute. Instead he stared at the crowd and began with a few lines that wowed the black-tie set: "Ladies and gentlemen. I am Head Hog." For that he received a standing ovation.

Shortly after earning their nickname, the Hogs donned tuxedos and tennis shoes and had a night out in Washington, D.C. Several of them walked into the Palm, where they stood out like . . . well . . . like a bunch of extra-large men wearing tuxedos would. "The manager said, 'If you take care of the food, we'll take care of the drink,'" center Jeff Bostic recalled. "He got the short end of that stick. We're in there and some lady bought us three bottles of Dom Perignon before we left. But offensive linemen don't drink Dom. She would have done better buying us a case of beer."

At old Redskins Park, a red shed sat near the practice field. After many practices, the Hogs would gather there to bond. Oh, and to drink beer—sometimes lots of it. "If we had to solve world problems, we'd be there two, three hours," Bostic said. "We would have been out there all day long if we had to deal with Iraq."

The shed's floor was crumbling. There was no air-conditioning, no heat, and no lights. They bought a kerosene heater but failed to operate it correctly at first, so, as Bostic said, "We all got smut up our nose. But we survived."

More important, others noticed the Hogs. Beer companies got involved, starting a mini tug-of-war for the Hogs' drinking affections. "It was real good when the Miller people and the Budweiser people were providing the beer," Bostic said.

"Anheuser-Busch was a friend to the guys on the line," tackle Joe Jacoby said.

Yes, the life of the Hogs was pretty good. Then again, the Hogs made life pretty good for the Redskins in the 1980s, earning a moniker that is forever embedded in the franchise's history. It started, the oft-told story goes, in training camp in 1982, when

*Redskins fans in their hog costumes at a game in 1984.* AP

offensive coordinator Joe Bugel shouted to his linemen, whose bellies bulged, "Okay, you Hogs, let's go down in the bullpen and hit those sleds." Bugel later handed out T-shirts with a razorback hog on the front to his group, and pretty soon an entire nation learned of the group's nickname, helped by the Redskins' success.

"The thing that worried me most when you get T-shirts for your guys is, how will the team react," Bugel said. "And the defense reacted well. They thought it was the greatest thing since sliced bread. I told them that everything's now in the paper, Hogs this and Hogs that and, boy, you'd better back up the nickname. That's why we put a lot of pressure on them. Even Joe [head coach Joe Gibbs] said the other teams are gonna say, 'We're

# A Hog's Life

Each of the original five Hogs has done well since his career ended. Joe Jacoby owns a car dealership, Jeff Bostic started a construction company, Mark May is a football analyst for ESPN, Russ Grimm is the Pittsburgh Steelers offensive coordinator, and George Starke, owner of Head Hog Barbecue Restaurant in Maryland, also founded the Excel Institute in Washington, D.C., a training facility for at-risk youth. (His image recently was tarnished when he was sentenced in July of 2004 to one year's probation and a $50 fine for drug possession.)

gonna butcher the Hogs.' We'd put that on the bulletin board—to say this is what they're thinking about you. Getting a nickname, getting T-shirts, it makes you perform a little better."

And pretty soon a cottage industry of Hogs followed. There were pig snouts and Head Hog Beer and a poster of the Hogs decked in tuxedos, top hats, and tennis shoes near a pig. There was a restaurant and Super Hogs, Inc. Men would attend games in dresses and pig snouts, calling themselves the Hogettes. They still go to games in those outfits, even though the Hogs' era unofficially ended when the last of the originals, Jacoby and Bostic, retired after the 1993 season.

Bostic's house was a Hog memorial, filled with ceramic pigs and crocheted pigs and even a pig made out of a coconut shell. "It's hard to believe," said Jacoby, who runs a car dealership now, "that I'm retired eleven years and it's like the Hogs' popularity hasn't faded or lost any luster from when we first started it. I get it every day. A guy came here the other day to buy a car and he said it [the Hogs' phenomenon] was the only reason he came here."

Throughout the NFL's history, the fancy nicknames belonged to other positions, usually the defensive line: the Fearsome Foursome, Purple People Eaters, Doomsday Defense, the Steel Curtain. And then came the Hogs, a collection of players whose fame would have been tough to predict in 1981.

There were castoffs such as Bostic, who joined the Redskins as a deep snapper in 1980. There was the undrafted, seemingly unwanted, Jacoby, who was once mistaken for a defensive tackle by coach Joe Gibbs. The coach chastised Bugel for wanting yet another offensive lineman in camp. They had too many already, Gibbs told him.

There were hotshots like first-round pick Mark May in 1981 and third-rounder Russ Grimm that same year, though it cost the Redskins a first-round pick in 1982 to trade up to select Grimm. And there was Starke, the seasoned pro already in his ninth season. Yet he, too, started ingloriously as an eleventh-round draft pick in 1971 who spent his first season on the taxi squad after getting traded once and cut twice.

They were joined as Hogs by tight ends Rick "Doc" Walker and Donnie Warren. Eventually running back John Riggins became an honorary Hog; quarterback Joe Theismann, much as they loved him, wasn't. He unsuccessfully petitioned to become a Hog. But they wanted to protect quarterbacks; they didn't want to mingle with them. Quarterbacks were upper class; Hogs were middle class.

While Starke was Head Hog—he incorporated Super Hogs after others outside the organization had already cashed in on the nickname—Bugel was Boss Hog. And Bugel is credited with whipping them into shape, turning them into the game's most famous offensive line. Not just because he came up with a nickname, but also because he tortured them in film sessions, yet wore out his hand patting them on the back during those same sessions.

Bugel arrived with Joe Gibbs in 1981, having already earned a reputation as one of the NFL's top line coaches. He was also intense and highly enthusiastic. Sometimes those made for a combustible situation. As an assistant at Western Kentucky in the 1960s, Bugel roomed with future NFL head coach Jerry Glanville.

Bugel was an offensive assistant, Glanville a defensive assistant. One day in practice, Glanville asked Bugel to help him demonstrate the bump-and-run technique. "So I came off the line, and he cut me," Bugel said. "I got up and whacked him. The players made a circle and we're out there fighting. We finally got in a clench and he says, 'I hope somebody breaks this up because I'm getting tired.'"

Any coach who would start a fight with another coach is a bit unusual—and intense. Bugel was both. But he knew there was only one way to mold a mostly young group into a strong, cohesive unit. "We tried to break them," Bugel said. "We put constant mental pressure on them in training camp, staying on them like a cheap suit. They planned to murder me. It was a lot of tough love. But I never overlooked anything. If you weren't running downfield or doing this, I stayed on them. I wouldn't let them come up for air. I tried to see how they would react. You have to find their hot button. Mark May, if you scolded him too much he would go into a shell. Grimm, you could kick him in the butt all day and he'd beg for more. Bostic and Jacoby were like that. The

*Offensive line coach Joe Bugel (right), the architect of the Hogs offensive line, over-sees a sled drill with two Redskins linemen.* Kevin Wolf/AP

more I got on them, the more they got tougher and tougher and tougher. It was a pride thing for them, 'He ain't running me off.'"

Every so often, Bugel would run his linemen hard the day after a game. It didn't matter if they had played well or not. "He could sense when we were getting cocky," said May. "He would surprise you and take you out and run you. Russ celebrated more than most after games. There were a lot of days he didn't make it [through the running]. It was a discipline act, but Joe did it because he knew that he had to do that to keep us in line."

Once, after a particularly bad game, Bugel asked for the T-shirts back. And defensive coaches, whose room was next to the offensive linemen's during that period, remembered hearing lots of yelling during film sessions. Sometimes it wasn't about anything the young Hogs had done wrong. "We're preparing for an upcoming opponent," Jacoby said, "and we're watching film and he's watching offensive line play. It's of another team. And he's getting upset watching their footwork. He gets mad, yelling and screaming at us about that. That's how intense he was. It was a love-hate relationship. Joe was very tough on you, but Joe also knew which individuals on the line he could be tough on and which ones he had to coddle to get them to play better. Sometimes he'd be in your face yelling and screaming and using very choice words. After that is over with and you make an outstanding play, he's the first one over there hugging you and telling you he loves you."

It wasn't just the yelling that got their attention. "Bugel took a bunch of young guys and taught them how to play the game," Bostic said. "He stressed technique, and we never got away from that. We had meetings after we were finished with film study. After we were done taking notes on what we were going to do, we'd walk through it. It was elementary education personified, and it was repetitive."

"One thing about them, they were super smart," Bugel said. "They had great football intelligence. You could explain something to them and they knew what you were talking about. You tell them one time and it was done. We were real fortunate to have those kinds of guys."

The linemen were smart enough to know Bugel was on their side, too. As much as he cajoled them, he also praised any good things they did. They considered him more of a father figure than a coach—he still talks to the original Hogs all the time. And when he left after the 1989 season to become the head coach of

The Hogs (from left): Mark May (73), offensive line coach Joe Bugel, Jeff Bostic (53), George Starke (in sunglasses), Russ Grimm (68), Joe Jacoby (66), and Rick "Doc" Walker (88). AP

the Arizona Cardinals, the Hogs, at a tearful party at Jacoby's house, presented him with a gold bracelet that had all their jersey numbers on it. Bugel said he'll be buried wearing that bracelet.

"We had a lot of fun together," Bugel said. "Our families liked each other and spent a lot of time together off the field. It was more than coach-player. It was like great friends, and great friends don't let each other down."

And now that Bugel is again coaching the offensive line for the Redskins, his new players, whom he's dubbed Dirtbags, noticed his impact, too. Before he suffered a season-ending Achilles injury, right tackle Jon Jansen talked about the little things Bugel would notice, things that hadn't been pointed out to him in the past.

# Bubba's Revenge

Trainer Bubba Tyer, who joined the organization in 1971, often kept players loose with practical jokes. He once got revenge on former Hog Russ Grimm, after the offensive lineman had thrown Tyer in the whirlpool for hiding his new case of chewing tobacco.

During practice later that day, as Grimm worked on the field, Tyer brought out Grimm's hat and clothes. As he waved to Grimm, he doused the pile with lighter fluid and then tossed in a match. The coaches played film of that before a late 1990s game at New York, making a point about revenge.

On one play in a training camp practice, Jansen's hand was lined up opposite the armpit of the defender. But Bugel pointed out as they watched film that his hand should have been lined up opposite the player's number. It's a 6-inch difference. Yet that's the difference between gaining leverage and not gaining leverage, which is the difference in getting beat or not getting beat. "That would not have been pointed out before as not good enough," Jansen said.

Bugel had talent to mold among the original Hogs, even if some of the players wound up to be surprises. And some ended up playing different positions. By the time Bugel had arrived, Starke was entrenched as a starter, even if his career began slowly. He was traded to Kansas City before the 1971 season and then was waived. So instead of playing, Starke was in Yonkers,

New York, teaching math and history. In the off-season, Dallas signed him and then cut him before training camp. Then the Redskins placed him on their taxi squad in 1972. Two years later he had earned a starting job.

Bostic arrived in 1980, after Philadelphia had released him. The Redskins weren't expecting much from him—he was just a deep snapper. He also lacked an imposing physique, earning the nickname "Doughboy" from his teammates because of his soft middle. "But we saw Bostic on special teams," Bugel said. "Here's a guy who's supposedly too small and too slow, but he'd get down there and make a lot of tackles. We said, 'That's a guy who deserves to play.'"

May and Grimm arrived from Pitt, both expected to contribute immediately. They did, just not at the positions anticipated. May was tried at left tackle and wound up starting that season at guard; Grimm was drafted to play center, but Bostic won that job so he was moved to guard.

The biggest surprise, though, was Jacoby, the 6'7", 300-pounder who was mistaken for a defensive lineman by Gibbs. Jacoby, who was extremely shy at the time, initially was too scared to correct his coach. But he impressed Bugel by holding his own against good-looking rookie end Dexter Manley in practice, despite a reputation for not being nimble of foot. Jacoby's play at left tackle helped May move to guard. "Joe had a great heart," Bugel said. "And he came in with a burr on his shoulder because he didn't get drafted. He had so much toughness."

He needed it: His mother died during training camp in 1981 and his father had already passed away, as had a younger brother, all from heart disease. "Nothing was ever easy for him," Bugel

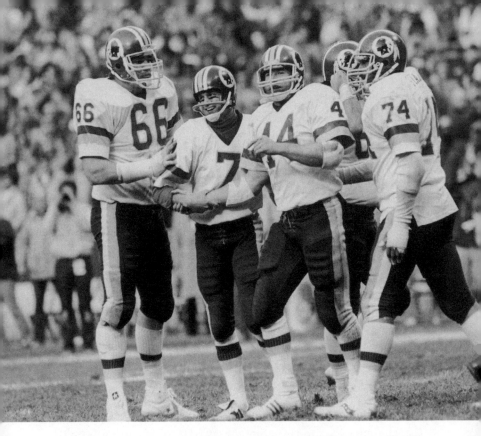

Quarterback Joe Theismann (7) celebrating a touchdown in 1983 with running back John Riggins (44) and Hogs Joe Jacoby (66) and George Starke (74). Scott Stewart/AP

said. "He got nothing for free, but that just made him stronger and stronger and the team loved him. When his momma passed away, he almost never came back. But our guys sent him money to fly him back, and they stayed on the telephone with him. They saved his life and his career. Those things right there, that made the team closer and closer."

The Hogs were a collection of characters, but what made them famous was their play. It started midway through the 1981 season, after a disastrous 0–5 start. The Redskins recovered to finish 8–8, thanks largely to the running of Riggins and the blocking of the line. In the strike-shortened 1982 season, the line established itself as a force in the playoffs. Riggins had games with 119, 185, and 140 yards rushing, then capped it off with a 166-yard effort in Washington's 27–17 victory over Miami in Super Bowl XVII.

A year later, Riggins ran for 24 touchdowns (an NFL record at the time). The popularity of the Hogs grew as the Redskins continued to play well, going 14–2 and reaching the Super Bowl again. When Starke drove around Tampa, site of the Super Bowl that season, he spotted banners hanging out of windows that read GO HOGS. "The results were great," Walker said. "The team won and we had a colorful coach in Bugel. But everything was about winning. None of this happens if we're not winning."

The line grew close: Jacoby and Grimm lived together in an apartment filled with pizza boxes, and they hung out often with Bostic and May. Starke, who would retire after the 1984 season, entertained at his bachelor pad. Walker, Warren, and Riggins were frequent visitors to the shed at Redskins Park. The players would vacation together as well.

That closeness also helped on the field, where in 1982 the starting five linemen missed a total of one game among them. During games, their line calls featured personal information. "We used our wives' names, then after a while we used our kids' names," Grimm said. "When our kids got older, it was time for us to retire."

The linemen weren't the only Redskins with nicknames during this period. There was also the "Fun Bunch" (and later the "Smurfs") for the receivers and "Diesel" for Riggins. But the Hogs outlasted them all. Two of the Hogs, Bostic and Jacoby, started for the Super Bowl championship teams in 1987 and 1991 as well. Grimm started in 1987 but was mostly a backup in 1991.

Grimm and Jacoby received the most accolades, both making the Pro Bowl four straight times from 1983 to 1986. Bostic earned a berth in 1983, May landed one in 1988, and Grimm landed a spot on the NFL's Team of the 1980s.

During this stretch, the Redskins won championships with three different starting quarterbacks and three different starting running backs. Meanwhile, the Hogs remained largely the same, though players such as Raleigh McKenzie, Mark Schlereth, Jim Lachey, and Ed Simmons became part of the group. However, the nucleus—and the soul—remained intact. "They had almost a ten-year span," said Walker, who retired after the 1985 season. "That was the thing that was unique. It wasn't just five, six, or seven players who defined it, but an entire unit."

This unit also made two plays famous: the Counter Trey in which the guard and tackle would pull, leading a back through the hole; and the appropriately named 50 Gut or 60 Gut, a straight-ahead, smashmouth run.

Despite their success, none of the Hogs is in the Pro Football Hall of Fame. Riggins is the only Redskins player from this era who has reached Canton. Gibbs also is enshrined. Jacoby and Grimm have the best shot from among the Hogs, but neither has been close. "It's disheartening to see that because of the success we had," Jacoby said, "and we don't have someone to represent us. But that's because of the group we had. We weren't big-name stars. We were no-names. We just did our job. How would you single out one of the offensive linemen over the others?"

They'd be happy if anyone else off those teams made the Hall of Fame. But in some ways it's appropriate that no one off this group is enshrined. "Sometimes," Bostic said, "the whole is better than the parts. And that was true of our group."

Besides, they won't need the Hall of Fame to be remembered. "It's amazing because that group will be remembered forever," Bugel said. "Especially in this town. When I walk through the airport, they say, 'There's the Hog coach.' They may not know my name, but they call me a Hog. They still remember. Anytime I meet someone from the old times, they remember that. That was a great offensive line, maybe one of the best ever to play in the NFL."

# Hidden Gems

No one predicted greatness for them, based on how they landed in Washington. They were low-round draft picks or out-of-work free agents just looking to impress someone. Anyone.

A number of players in Redskins history have blossomed as free agents or low-round picks. But four players stand out as true hidden gems because of what they achieved after entering pro football with little fanfare.

"The Redskins had their offices at Ninth and H," recalled center Len Hauss, who was a ninth-round draft pick in 1964. "I came up to Washington on the train, got a cab to the Redskins office. There were eight or nine of us standing around, and we didn't talk to each other. A guy came out and took us on a bus to Carlisle [to training camp]." Thus began a standout career in which Hauss made the Pro Bowl six times with Washington. Like Hauss, each of these other hidden gems made multiple Pro Bowls or were named players of the year.

## Len Hauss

Midway through his first training camp in 1964, with a knee swelling a little more each day, a group of linemates ignoring him, and his chances of making the roster, in his mind, slim, Hauss had only one thought. He wanted to quit. And if not for trainer Joe Kuczo, the best center in Redskins history might have left for another career. Though Hauss was annoyed by other factors, it was a knee injury suffered in college that bothered him most. He told no one except Kuczo, who talked Hauss into staying.

"I'd go into the training room and say, 'I don't think I have a dog's chance,'" Hauss recalled. "Joe would say, 'Len, you worry about your play, I'll worry about your knee, and we'll get through it.' He was a big factor in my success. He was very encouraging. If I got an injury, I would try to hide the fact, figuring a rookie had a hard enough time making it, and if he had a bad knee that would be a real strike." Next thing Hauss knew, he was embarking on a fourteen-year NFL career. His six Pro Bowls were the most ever by a Redskins lineman.

Not that Hauss, who was drafted out of Georgia, anticipated such success. He always rented a house in the Washington area, never feeling secure enough to buy, and he returned to Georgia in the off-season. By the time Hauss grew comfortable with the fact that he would be a Redskin for a while, he was accustomed to his arrangement.

That first camp, however, was difficult. He joined a line on which most of the starters had played together for several years. They viewed him as someone trying to take either their job or the job of a friend. "It was like, 'Who's that kid, and why is he here?'" Hauss said. "None of those guys would talk to me. I don't think I talked to someone for the first two weeks I was there. It was a cold atmosphere and a lonely time. If it sounds like my career was a bed of roses, it really wasn't."

However, he also came to the right team, which he would soon discover. Though the line had been together, they had reason to be paranoid. It wasn't as if the Redskins had been any good, having won a combined ten games the previous four seasons. Also, Washington had traded for quarterback Sonny Jurgensen that same off-season. The Redskins would need better pass blockers. Hauss was small, weighing just 225 pounds (though he would tape two-and-a-half-pound weights, hidden underneath his sweats, to his ankles during weigh-ins). But he was quick. And after three games, the coaches tired of seeing Jurgensen get pummeled. "Sonny was getting torn up," Hauss said, "and I'd imagine that he went back to the coaches and said, 'Hey, if we can't pick up a blitz, they're going to kill us.' So they gave me a shot."

His first start came against the St. Louis Cardinals, a team, Hauss said, that lived and died by the blitz, led by middle linebacker Dale Meinert. The Cardinals recorded no sacks in that game. The Redskins still lost 23–17, but they won six of the next ten games to finish 6–8. "Every time they blitzed, I was able to pick up the linebacker," Hauss said. "I was smaller than a lot of centers, but I had quickness and speed to pick up those blitzing linebackers. Or if a defensive lineman came free, I could pick him up. I was good at that."

Hauss was good at a lot of things, which is why he remained the starting center through the 1977 season, making the Pro Bowl each season from 1967 to 1972. And it wouldn't have happened had Hauss not been talked into staying. "It certainly was never easy," Hauss said. "But it was surprising that it went so well."

## Chris Hanburger

When the games started, the last place linebacker Chris Hanburger wanted to be was stuck in the crowd. Barely more than 200 pounds, he couldn't survive there. So he avoided blockers, delivering a false step to his left, then darting back the other way toward the ball. It worked: No other Redskins player made more Pro Bowls.

When the games ended, the last place Hanburger wanted to be was stuck in the crowd. So he avoided restaurants, movie theaters, and even some buses. That worked, too: Hanburger maintained his sanity by relaxing with his family. "That's just me," Hanburger said.

And that was just fine with the Redskins. If it bothered teammates that he avoided crowds off the field, it certainly didn't bother them that he avoided them on the field. That helped the former eighteenth-round pick from North Carolina make nine

Pro Bowls in his fourteen seasons from 1965 to 1978. He was the NFC defensive player of the year in 1972.

Even now, however, Hanburger isn't quite sure why he had such a standout career. But his actions provide all the evidence. The undersized Hanburger was quicker and smarter than most, and he improved as he aged, helped by film study. Considering he was small, that quickness was needed. To make himself seem bigger, he'd also tape two-and-a-half pound weights to his body on weigh-in day, boosting him up to 218 pounds. "Shucks, I'd go to camp at 215 and halfway through the season I'd be down to 200, 205," he said. If the coaches knew, they weren't going to stop this practice, especially not once Hanburger started to play. By his second season, he'd already earned a Pro Bowl berth.

"It was my quickness more than anything else," Hanburger said. "Certainly I couldn't take people on, so I had to try and set up blockers so they missed me."

But he was also disciplined, thanks to a military background. His father served in the army as an engineer and a pilot. And Hanburger spent two years in the military before attending North Carolina. That trait came in handy in the 1970s under coach George Allen. Before then Hanburger relied on smarts and athletic ability to survive. Under Allen the defense was more complex. Allen wanted his middle linebacker to be the defensive quarterback. So Hanburger had to know the defense inside and out, the same way he had to know the opponent. And that meant lots of film study. "Before then, I'd never thought to ask to take film home, and it was never offered," Hanburger said.

Allen changed that. Hanburger would meet with Allen during the week, before practices, in team meetings, and in defensive meetings. Hanburger would sit in on sessions with the

Linebacker Chris Hanburger (55) blitzing in a 1978 game against the Baltimore Colts. AP

defensive backs and the defensive linemen. And he'd watch more film at home Tuesday through Friday.

The film study helped. Hanburger picked up on players' tendencies, noticing where they'd align their hands on runs or passes. He remembered one tackle who would drag his hand back when he was going to pass-block. On a run, the tackle wouldn't move his hand once he was set. An undersized player seeks every advantage, and that's what Hanburger did. "I just became a better student of the game," Hanburger said. "It's amazing the things you can pick up. I learned very quickly that it was a tremendous advantage."

After missing the Pro Bowl in 1970 and 1971, Hanburger made it the next five seasons. This from a guy who didn't want his wife to move to Washington during his first training camp. "I didn't know how long I would last," he said. Turns out he lasted fourteen years. He liked to be alone off the field, but he was always a part of the action on the field.

## Larry Brown

The story is part of Redskins legend and bears repeating. In 1969 Vince Lombardi noticed rookie Larry Brown would get a slow start off the ball and thought something was wrong. So he had Brown examined by a hearing specialist, who recommended a hearing aid. Brown had known since elementary school that his hearing wasn't good. But he ignored it, and no one noticed anything amiss until Lombardi stepped in and made the suggestion that would alter Redskins history. The hearing aid became one of the most important pieces of equipment in Washington.

There was only one problem. The hearing aid didn't always work. Though he always had it on during games, it couldn't withstand the punishment. "Initially it helped a lot," Brown said. "I realized somewhere during the first few games I had it that it wasn't functioning 100 percent. There were times it wasn't working, and it became more of a problem than a benefit."

Just as important was where Lombardi had Brown stand in the huddle. Instead of being on the opposite side of the quarterback, as was typical for a back, he moved Brown next to quarterback Sonny Jurgensen, allowing him to hear the play better. This, coupled with the hearing aid, allowed the rookie eighth-round pick from Kansas State to flourish. During that first camp, Lombardi told Jurgensen

# Six-for-Six

Larry Brown led the Redskins in rushing for six consecutive seasons from 1969 to 1974. That's the longest such streak in franchise history.

| Year | Rushes | Yards | Average | Touchdowns |
|------|--------|-------|---------|------------|
| 1969 | 202 | 888 | 4.4 | 4 |
| 1970 | 237 | 1,125 | 4.8 | 5 |
| 1971 | 253 | 948 | 3.7 | 4 |
| 1972 | 285 | 1,216 | 4.3 | 8 |
| 1973 | 273 | 860 | 3.2 | 8 |
| 1974 | 163 | 430 | 2.6 | 3 |

that Brown "would be around a long time."

It also helped that Brown was tough, fast, and one heck of a runner. The Redskins record book provides the evidence: Brown is number two on the franchise's all-time list with 5,875 yards rushing on 1,530 carries. This from a guy who didn't start playing football until his junior year of high school and was a blocking fullback at Kansas State. "I was at the right place at the right time," Brown said. "My only limitation was that I didn't have a track record of catching passes, but I could block. The blocking and the toughness were there in the beginning."

Lombardi rode Brown hard. He taught him how to finish runs, placing a towel on the ground 20 yards from the line of scrimmage during practice; Brown had to run to that point after every play. And once, Brown was tackled and put the ball on the ground. Lombardi thought he had fumbled and chastised Brown, who dared tell the coach that he didn't fumble. Brown quickly learned that only one opinion in that conversation was right. And it wasn't his. Lombardi ordered him to carry a football everywhere he went for a week. "It was a way of humiliating me in front of my teammates," Brown said, "but also making that a priority. It was embarrassing. No one likes to be the brunt of jokes for a week. But after a few days, you couldn't do anything but laugh. . . . At that point I thought I had won him over. I realized that when a guy has to make up a mistake for you, then you must be doing things right."

However, Brown still had to show he could catch. That wasn't happening in practice. Then, in a preseason game, Brown recalled being a primary target. This time, Brown caught everything. "Vince came over to me and said, 'Why can't you catch in practice?'" Brown said. "I told him, 'You put more pressure on me in practice than 80,000 fans in the stands do.' That went over well."

Lombardi then put fear into Brown's running style. The Hall of Fame coach told Brown he could stray from the intended hole, as long as he didn't take a loss. Thus developed Brown's darting style to go with the toughness of an ex-fullback. "I learned very soon that looking for another hole could be bad for one's health," Brown said. "I knew if I was looking for an alternate route, I didn't have a lot of time to screw around trying to make that decision."

Lombardi might have ignited Brown's career, but it was coach George Allen who eventually profited from Brown, riding him to the Super Bowl in 1972 (two years after he led the NFL in rushing with 1,125 yards). That season Brown rushed for an NFC-best 1,216 yards, caught 32 passes for 473 yards, and scored 12 touchdowns. When he retired, Brown was Washington's all-time leading rusher and ranked third on the team's all-time list

*Running back Larry Brown being brought down in the rain during a game with the Chicago Bears in 1969.* AP

with 55 touchdowns, including 35 on the ground. He also caught 238 passes for 2,485 yards.

For years, Brown's supporters have lobbied that he should be in the Pro Football Hall of Fame. His numbers are borderline—the touchdowns are far short of other modern-day backs in Canton. Leroy Kelly, a contemporary of Brown's, was inducted in 1994 after retiring in 1973 with 90 touchdowns and 12,329 combined yards. On the other hand, the Redskins' attack revolved around Brown. This number matters most to his ex-teammates: 71–38–3 (including 53–28–3 when he was the primary runner). That's Washington's won-loss record with Brown.

"I don't think about it as much as friends of mine do," Brown said. "I don't know what the rule is for getting in. They say it's your contribution to the game. Okay, my contribution to the game is based on my Redskins' contributions. If it's significant, then that should make my contribution to the NFL significant."

Brown's contributions to the Redskins ensure him a place among their all-time greats. "I've never seen anyone work as hard in practice as he did," former Redskins defensive tackle Bill Brundige said. "He was just nasty. He was hell on wheels."

## Mark Moseley

The players spotted him in front of the mirror as they walked in from practice. Their bodies were covered in mud, their breath visible in the cold air. And there stood the kicker, poking at his hair and putting powder on his body.

So they took action, led by defensive tackle Dave Butz. The next thing Mark Moseley knew, he was being dragged through a puddle of mud and water by laughing teammates. "My nature was that I had thick skin so everyone used to bounce jokes off me, and I took it," Moseley said. "But I told them, 'It took five offensive and defensive linemen to drag me through the mud.'"

They may have ragged on Moseley, but they also depended on him. And Moseley rarely let them down. By the time he was finished with his twelve and a half seasons in Washington, Moseley was the only kicker ever to be named NFL MVP. He also was the best kicker in Redskins history, a distinction he still owns.

Thing is, Moseley was only in Washington because of one game in 1972—when he played for Houston—and because his old coach had a dream, prompting him to cut the young kicker. Houston coach Bill Peterson dreamt that his quarterback/punter

Dan Pastorini was injured, leaving him without a punter. So after the season opener he cut Moseley and signed someone who could handle both jobs.

That forced Moseley to the sidelines for nearly three seasons, during which he dug septic tanks, worked in real estate, and took classes. He also added twenty pounds of muscle. He even tried to make himself more marketable by working on his punting—with his left foot. And he kicked every day, often with his wife, Sharon, as his holder. By the time he signed with Washington in 1974, Moseley was more than ready to excel. And the Redskins needed someone who could kick in all sorts of weather on a sometimes messy and soft field.

Moseley long ago had proven he could kick in any conditions. At Livingston High School in Texas, where he also starred at running back and once scored 8 touchdowns in a game, Moseley routinely kicked on fields that once were cow pastures. "The fields in the NFL were like someone's manicured front yard compared to what I played in growing up," Moseley said.

In 1971 he booted two field goals in a driving rainstorm at RFK Stadium while playing for Houston, kicks that turned out to be the most important in Washington's history. Three years later, when George Allen needed a kicker, he remembered that game, found out who the kicker was, and signed him—without a tryout. Moseley figured he was fine, until he arrived in camp and saw twelve other kickers competing for the same position, including incumbent Curt Knight.

Moseley won the job. Then he nearly blew it in the first game, against the St. Louis Cardinals. Right before halftime, Moseley missed two field goals in five seconds. He missed the first one, got a second chance because of a penalty, and missed again. "I just knew George was going to cut me," Moseley said. "But I had a good special teams coach [Paul Lanham]. George asked him if he should replace me, and he said no." Wise move. Moseley eventually made the Pro Bowl in 1979 and again in 1982, his MVP season. But he nearly was cut before that season. Following a sluggish 1980—Moseley made just 18 of 33 field-goal attempts—the Redskins started searching for a replacement. After a 19-for-30 season in 1981, Washington drafted Dan Miller in the eleventh round. "They told him the job was his, so I came in expecting to be cut," Moseley said. "But I made up my mind that I would fight for it."

Mental toughness was a Moseley strength, evidenced by his missing only one potential game-winning kick in his thirteen-year career with the Redskins (a 39-yarder in a 48–47 loss at Green Bay in 1983). He excelled in adverse conditions: He had one of his best seasons in 1979, the year his sister was raped and murdered; and he never used his wife's cancer surgery in 1980 as an excuse.

In the preseason finale, with the competition even, Miller missed two short field goals in the first half and another one in the third quarter. Moseley wasn't supposed to kick on this night, but second-year coach Joe Gibbs called him over as the Redskins drove late in the game, wanting to know if he would kick.

Moseley kicked a game-winning 51-yarder to clinch the job. In the season opener, he kicked a game-tying field goal and then won it in overtime to beat Philadelphia. Miller was cut and Moseley went on to complete a then-record 23 in a row, dating to the previous season. In 1982 he missed only once in 21 attempts. "My MVP year, I was very lucky to be on the team," he said.

But Moseley felt the Redskins weren't crazy about him being the MVP. "In the press guide it was, 'Oh, by the way, Mark was

# Record Kicker

Nearly twenty years after he last played for the Redskins, former kicker Mark Moseley still holds a number of club records. Among them:

| | |
|---|---|
| Most Points, Career | 1,207 |
| Most Points, Season | 161 (1983) |
| Most Points After Touchdown, Career | 417 |
| Most Points After Touchdown, Season | 62 (1983) |
| Most Points After Touchdown Attempts, Career | 442 |
| Most Points After Touchdown Attempts, Season | 63 (1983) |
| Most Field Goals, Career | 263 |
| Most Field Goals, Season | 33 (1983) |
| Most Field Goals, Game* | 5 (versus Saints, 1980) |
| Most Field Goal Attempts, Career | 397 |
| Most Consecutive Field Goals | 23 (1981–82) |
| Most Consecutive Field Goals, Season | 20 (1982) |
| Best Field-Goal Percentage, Season (minimum 20 attempts) | .952 (20 of 21, 1982) |

*Shares record

MVP,'" Moseley said. "I didn't think about it, but I thought it was kind of strange. In a way, I understand it. There was a lot of pride in the fact that we were supposed to have this great offense and we didn't, and a kicker had to win the games for us."

Moseley also wonders if he belongs in the Hall of Fame, where Jan Stenerud is the only pure kicker in Canton. Moseley, one of the last straight-on kickers, finished as the NFL's fourth all-time leading scorer. "I started changing the way people look at kickers," he said. "I always thought it was strange that I didn't get a little bit more accolades. But I don't dwell on it."

The Redskins cut him in 1986, a move Moseley, who was 6 of 12 at the time, believes was helped by the departure of his longtime holder, Joe Theismann. Jay Schroeder replaced Theismann and, Moseley said, "was terrible."

But Moseley didn't let that spoil his Redskins memories. And he didn't fret over whether or not others considered him "just a kicker." Moseley considered himself a football player. He played quarterback and cornerback at Stephen F. Austin and played semipro ball after he retired. He still remembers his biggest hits on kick coverage. However, it's his kicks that made him a huge part of Redskins history. "A lot of players end up somewhere by luck or by fate," Moseley said. "Players are made for certain areas. I happened to be made for the Redskins."

# Capital Gains: Best Acquisitions

In the mid-1960s, the Redskins decided they needed a big running back. So they traded for Joe Don Looney, the talented but troubled runner. And they paid linebacker Sam Huff $1,000 to room with him, hoping Huff's guidance would keep Looney straight.

It didn't work: Huff hated him and the two engaged in a fistfight in practice their second year, two days before a game. Looney was soon cut. "That was awful, absolutely awful," Huff said. "I couldn't go through that again. He needed more help than I could give him. And we had a hell of a fight. We duked it out. I knocked him down, but he didn't stay down."

Other trades, however, worked out much better for Washington, fueling the Redskins' twenty-year run of success.

## Pat Fischer

A lasting image still provides a chuckle for his former teammates. In the dugout before games, Pat Fischer would take one last drag on a cigarette just before getting introduced. As he raced out of the dugout, teammates noticed something unusual coming from his helmet. "On cold days, he'd come up out of the dugout and the smoke would come through his ear holes," former defensive tackle and teammate Diron Talbert said, "and it looked like he was on fire."

Fischer claims the story is wildly exaggerated. Other players recall Fischer using stickum, getting the sticky substance on his mouthpiece, and then drooling. Fischer claimed it only happened once. That hardly matters to his teammates. What mattered more was his play, and Fischer excelled from the time Washington acquired him via trade from St. Louis in 1968 until he retired after the 1977 season. He remained a starter until undergoing season-ending back surgery in his final year.

Fischer made the Pro Bowl in 1969 and earned second-team All-Pro honors in 1972. He intercepted 27 passes with Washington and 56 overall in his seventeen-year career, which started as a seventeenth-round pick out of Nebraska in 1961. By the time he was finished, Fischer had set an NFL record for games played by a cornerback, a mark that stood until another Redskin, Darrell Green, broke it.

Like Green, Fischer survived a big man's game despite a small man's frame. He stood only 5'9", yet he never shied from contact and routinely handled tall receivers such as Philadelphia's 6'8" Harold Carmichael and fast ones such as Dallas's "Bullet" Bob Hayes.

Fischer thrived because he was tough and prepared. Even now, he says, he can close his eyes and picture routes run by receivers he used to cover. He can picture how they lined up, how they took their first step, and how they came out of their breaks. And he loved being challenged. "When you're in a critical part of the game, throw it over here," he said. "Throw it to Bob Hayes or Harold Carmichael because he's not gonna catch it."

Fischer's size disadvantage didn't worry him because he knew he could tackle anyone, such as the time he stuffed burly Green Bay fullback John Burlington often during a 1972 playoff game. It was just a matter of figuring out where to attack. That's what he did his whole life, dating to his youth in St. Edwards, Nebraska. "I was always an angry kid," he said. "I knew I was good, I don't know why. And I knew I could tackle people. The first time I was ever out on a Little League team, I tackled this big guy, and I was so proud of myself that I could do that. The success fed on itself."

And the stories fed on themselves. Teammates knew his love of nicotine, an affair that started when Fischer was a kid, smoking cigars in the third or fourth grade. Before games he'd down a pot of coffee and then smoke. "He was feisty, a banny rooster kind of guy," Talbert said. "I loved him to death. He was always fired up and ready to go."

# Ken Houston

Something caused him to call for another defense—a gut feeling by the All-Pro safety. Something told Chris Hanburger, who was calling the signals, to pay attention. Next thing they knew, Ken Houston had forever claimed a spot in Redskins lore. All he did was stop a ballcarrier at the goal line of a 7-point game in the final seconds. And this made it more dramatic: It was against Dallas in 1973, and it was on a Monday night, giving the entire nation a chance to witness the most famous tackle in Redskins history. "After that play, I remember George saying that was enough to justify the trade," Houston said.

Oh yes, the trade. A five-for-one swap (Houston was the one) with the Oilers in 1973 that turned out to be a steal—for Washington. The Oilers didn't like Houston serving as a union representative and used a minicontract squabble as an opportunity to trade him. "The trade was traumatic," Houston said.

He wasn't an instant starter in Washington. Instead, coach George Allen worked him with the second string behind Brig Owens and Roosevelt Taylor, until Taylor broke an arm. Then Owens was moved to free safety and Houston became the starting strong safety. "I'm thinking, he traded for me, I'll be a starter," Houston said. "Then I realized George's philosophy was you don't lose a position, somebody takes it."

Houston took it all right, making a living out of big plays like the one on October 8, 1973, against Dallas. With the Redskins leading, 14–7, Dallas faced fourth-and-goal from the 6 yard line with twenty-four seconds to play. In the huddle, Hanburger called a play only to be told by Houston, "Call another." For one of the few times, maybe the only time, Hanburger changed the call based on another player's suggestion.

*Ken Houston made seven straight Pro Bowls while playing for Washington.* AP

Houston wanted a defense that had him covering the running back, not the tight end as he usually would. Good move. Quarterback Craig Morton rolled right and threw to running back Walt Garrison at the goal line. Few in the RFK Stadium crowd of more than 55,000 doubted he would score. But Houston wouldn't let him.

Initially, Houston thought he could intercept the ball. "If I had intercepted the ball and run it [back] for a touchdown, it would have been just another play," Houston said. "But I hear about it all the time now. I'll hear from Cowboys fans and they'll say, 'You made me lose money on that Monday night game.'"

Houston remembered yelling for Owens to help him, thinking that Garrison might try and lateral the ball. He also remembers silence. "It was like I was the only voice on the field and everyone else was holding their breath and waiting for it to happen," Houston said. "No one said a word. Then when everyone realized what had happened, it got louder and louder and louder."

But that wasn't Houston's lone highlight against Dallas. One year later, subbing for an injured returner, he ran back a punt 58 yards for a touchdown. In 1975 he intercepted a Roger Staubach pass in overtime, setting up the game-winning touchdown.

There was more. In 1978 Houston intercepted a pass in the end zone to preserve Washington's 9–5 victory. And in 1979 he forced Staubach to fumble on a blitz late in the first half, with Dallas on the 3 yard line and trailing 14–3. "It seemed like when I played Dallas I got on another level," said Houston, a Texas native. "I really got caught up in the George Allen hype. You didn't want to go home and lose to Dallas. You'd hear about it for six months."

Such plays helped Houston make seven straight Pro Bowls with Washington. He retired with a then-NFL record 9 interception returns for a touchdown (it's now second).

Houston's success was hard to predict. He was a high school center who earned a scholarship to Prairie View because the school wanted to sign a friend of his. Houston was nearly cut at Prairie View, until he was moved to defense as a last chance. And the Oilers didn't draft him until the ninth round in 1967. In his first training camp, he twice tried to quit.

It was also hard to figure him out. On the field, Houston earned a label as a big hitter. "I would clothesline a guy, but that was legal," Houston said. "They didn't like it, but that's the way it was."

Off the field no one was more peaceful. Once during a flood in Houston, he carried toddlers home from nursery school on his shoulders. At his home he stocked his lake with fish and then grew too fond of them. When friends came to fish, Houston would make them throw back anything they caught. He earned humanitarian awards. He was named Washington's man of the year twice. He won the Bart Starr Meritorious Award.

"Kenny didn't smoke, drink, or swear," former Redskins defensive lineman Bill Brundige said. "He was a Christian fellow, had a super-intelligent wife, and was soft-spoken. He was the nicest guy you'd ever want to meet in your entire life. But when he got on the field, he was vicious."

## Dave Butz

As he attempted to roll off an X-ray table, Dave Butz snuck a peek at his injured knee. Bad move. The knee was bent at a 90-degree angle. Even for a tough defensive tackle, that's hard to see. "I screamed," Butz said. "The nurse turned around and picked it back up on the table because I couldn't do it." Doctors told the second-year player that his career could be over. Not only that, but they predicted the 1973 all-rookie performer might never run again.

Fourteen weeks later, Butz returned to the practice field. One year later, the St. Louis Cardinals traded the free agent defensive tackle's rights to Washington. Clearly the Redskins thought he could play. In 1975 they sent their number-one picks in 1977 and 1978 and a second-rounder in 1979 to land him. "I thought that was way too much to give up," Butz said, "because the Cardinals told me they didn't think I could play. If they thought I couldn't play, they shouldn't have gotten that much."

It turned out to be a one-sided deal as none of the picks panned out for St. Louis. Meanwhile, Butz played fourteen seasons for Washington, anchoring the defensive middle during the 1980s. He was voted to only one Pro Bowl, in 1983, but he often occupied two blockers, allowing others to succeed.

Injuries limited Butz early in his Redskins career. He missed six games with a sprained ankle in 1977 and didn't start for an entire season until 1978. Veterans teased him endlessly, questioning his toughness. They should have seen him between 1980 and 1988 when Butz missed only one game, because of food poisoning. The night before a 1987 game against the Jets, Butz spent the night in the hospital hooked to an IV pumping him with eleven quarts of fluid. He left the hospital at 9:00 A.M., recorded a sack, received a game ball for his efforts, and returned to the hospital for another round of IVs. That week, an intestinal disorder caused him to lose twenty-four pounds, yet he never missed a practice or a meeting.

Another time, in 1986, Butz broke his thumb in the first half of a game against the Raiders. Against the wishes of his wife, Candyce, Butz played the second half with a cast. Two 3½-inch pins were drilled from his thumb to the bone. He never missed a game. "When I got hit in the pins and the pins were in the bone, it didn't feel good," he said.

There was also the time at the Pro Bowl when Butz battled a virus. He needed help from Dallas's Randy White just to make it to the bus. Butz took some medication, received a shot, spent part of the game going back and forth to the bathroom—and recorded two and a half sacks.

"And my last year I played with a sprained ankle," Butz said. "It never healed. The only way I could go was straight ahead. Some people thought, 'Dave's lost a step and has gotten old.' They forgot about the amount of taping it took just to get me out there to play."

Former teammate Pat Fischer said, "He developed into a courageous teammate. I don't think anyone would have guessed that from the first year or two he was here."

And there was constant debate about how good the 6'7", 300-pound Butz was—should he dominate more, considering he was, as former Dallas center John Gesek said, "as big as a house"? But as former teammate Russ Grimm said, Butz was someone the Redskins could count on. Butz knew that, which is why he rarely left the field even when injured. "That's just the way I am," Butz said. "I just feel like I was paid to play; but hell yes, it was difficult to do it."

## John Riggins

First, a story about John Riggins from Joe Bugel: "He was crazy. Anyone who went bowling naked with a pair of cowboy boots on, you have to be a little bit touched. But he could do it. They shut down the bowling alley, and he's in there by himself."

That's just a start. There was also the time he told Supreme Court Justice Sandra Day O'Connor at a function to "loosen up, Sandy baby." There was the time head coach Joe Gibbs showed up at his home in Lawrence, Kansas, trying to persuade Riggins to return to football. Riggins answered the door holding a beer. It was 9:00 A.M. "I don't think Joe was pleased with that," Riggins later said.

"I got through meeting with him and walked out and said, 'Oh my goodness,'" Gibbs recalled.

That's probably tamer than what Gibbs thought when Riggins reportedly missed a team meeting the night before a playoff game against Minnesota in 1983, presumably because he was out partying. The next day he asked his linemen not to open big holes because "I don't want to get 10 or 15 yards downfield and make a fool of myself by falling down."

"He was a fun-loving guy," former Redskins general manager Charley Casserly said. "Any story you hear about him is true, and I don't even know what the story is. He had wild times, no question about that."

Riggins would show up in camp with a goatee one year or a shaved head the next. One year, with the Jets, he donned a Mohawk. He'd ride his motorcycle from Kansas to training camp in Carlisle, Pennsylvania. But there's a danger in trying to portray Riggins as simply someone who drank, was outrageous, and was comical. Those aren't the reasons he stuck around.

"Come Sunday," Casserly said, "the guy was something." Come Sunday he was special. More than anything that's why Riggins is remembered—and why he's in the Pro Football Hall of

Fame. Riggins remains the Redskins all-time leader in rushing (7,472 yards) and rushing touchdowns (79).

And the bigger the game the more impressive the effort. In the 1982 playoffs, Riggins rushed for 444 yards in three games, including 185 in that win over Minnesota. Then he gave Washington a 20–17 lead over Miami late in Super Bowl XVII with a 43-yard touchdown run, part of his record 166-yard performance.

Riggins combined strength with speed. When the Jets drafted him in the first round in 1971 out of Kansas, Riggins was dubbed the white Jim Brown. But in 1976 the players' union and the league had not yet agreed on a contract, making some players free agents for a brief period. The Redskins capitalized by signing Riggins (along with two Dallas starters, running back Calvin Hill and tight end Jean Fugett).

Initially Riggins served as a blocking back for Mike Thomas. Riggins stopped doing interviews in 1977, depressed over his role. Once, the night before a game, Riggins called his brother Billy and told him to check out his fashion statement the next day. "I'm gonna have a doughnut around my neck," he said in his autobiography. "I'm gonna have a lineman's shoulder pads, high tops, all the padding. If they want me to block, be a lineman, then I'm gonna dress like one."

Because Riggins was paid $300,000 a season, *Sports Illustrated* labeled him in 1977 as "one of the most overpaid players in pro sports." His season ended after five games because of a knee injury. Two unsatisfactory seasons later (though he rushed for a combined 2,167 yards) Riggins had had enough, and he sat out the 1980 season. For a guy with his reputation, he stayed in excellent shape by digging ditches, chopping wood, and working out at the University of Kansas—always during nonpeak hours to avoid attention.

*John Riggins eludes a Miami Dolphins tackler in Super Bowl XVII.* AP

Shortly after Gibbs's two-hour visit, he returned to the Redskins and into history. But his initial ride with Gibbs wasn't smooth, either. After three games, Gibbs said Riggins had played poorly and might be finished. Two games later, Riggins became the focal point of Washington's offense, helping spur eight wins in the final eleven weeks.

But Riggins's legacy was cemented in the 1982 postseason. He asked Bugel to tell Gibbs he wanted the ball. Bugel told Riggins to tell Gibbs himself. The two rarely talked, but Riggins went to him this time with his request. "I don't figure I'll have many of these chances left," Riggins said.

"You've got it," Gibbs told him.

Four straight 100-yard games produced four straight wins and a Super Bowl trophy. Late in one of those games, a 21–7 victory over Minnesota, Gibbs sent a replacement in for Riggins, knowing he'd get a standing ovation as he ran off the field. What he didn't expect was this: Riggins bowing to the crowd.

A year later, Riggins spit up blood during halftime of a playoff game against San Francisco. He stayed in the game, rushed for 123 yards, and scored two touchdowns. There's a reason he's the only Hog who wasn't a lineman. "He was a big-game guy," Gibbs said. "I never had a problem with him. Every now and then I'd have a conversation with him about his wild, man-about-town stuff. But he was a great team guy. He was a guy who was on the stage of life."

"Joe didn't know how to deal with him," former Redskins defensive end Charles Mann said. "He just kind of left him alone. That was the thorn in Joe's side. If Riggo wasn't getting it done, he would have been one of Gibbs's first cuts. But Riggins respected him and was fearful of Gibbs. And on game day, he was a beast."

During the 1984 season, Riggins saved his best for the last month, helping secure a playoff berth. Washington needed to win the final two games to make the playoffs. Riggins had been in and out of the lineup with a bad back. Two days before facing Dallas in the fifteenth game, Riggins was in traction at the hospital. He rushed for 111 yards and a touchdown in a 30–28 win. He returned to the hospital, going into traction again, and played in the finale, a 29–27 victory over St. Louis in which he carried twenty-seven times for 76 yards.

"The guy was thirty-five," Casserly said in wonderment twenty years later. "In training camp, he'd be the last guy off the

## Riggo's Run

John Riggins's run through the 1982 postseason was one of the most remarkable in NFL history. Here's what he did, game-by-game:

| Opponent | Attempts | Yards | Average | TDs | Result |
|----------|----------|-------|---------|-----|--------|
| Detroit | 25 | 199 | 8.0 | 0 | Redskins won, 31–7 |
| Minnesota | 37 | 185 | 5.0 | 1 | Redskins won, 21–7 |
| Dallas | 36 | 140 | 3.9 | 2 | Redskins won, 31–17 (NFC title game) |
| Miami | 38 | 166 | 4.4 | 1 | Redskins won, 27–17 (Super Bowl XVII) |
| Totals | 136 | 690 | 5.1 | 4 | |

field. I remember sometimes Joe would give him the afternoons off and he'd train on his own. He'd work harder training on his own than the other guys practicing."

"He'd be on one of the other fields working with [strength coach] Dan Riley," former lineman Joe Jacoby said, "and he'd do 10, 20, 100-yard sprints. He would sit in the meeting rooms with us to see the same things we were seeing. He knew how the holes would be and how we would block."

But it always returns to stories of his escapades. Early in the week before Super Bowl XVII, Riggins and a few of the linemen went out drinking, waking up teammates upon their return early in the morning. A few days later he attended a Redskins administrative party decked out in a top hat and tails. "He was so unconventional, and I think that was by design," said Don Breaux, then the Redskins running-backs coach. "He'd give you the impression that he was some old country bumpkin out of Kansas, and he was anything but that. He'd quote Shakespeare out there. He always surprised you."

But he was always noticed, particularly by teammates. "If he did something, everyone followed," Mann said. "He was a big hunter, and he wore all this camouflage stuff with cowboy boots. He'd wear camouflage shorts and cowboy boots. Next thing you know others are trying to do it. They were always trying to copy him."

That wasn't always a good thing. "There were teammates who'd go out with Riggo but couldn't do what he did on Sunday," said trainer Bubba Tyer, who disliked the way some in the organization enabled Riggins's habits. "They wouldn't play as well or show up on time for practice, and their careers were cut short."

Those escapades are remembered as much as his play. One without the other would have made him memorable. Both together have made him unforgettable. "He was John Wayne," Casserly said. "John Wayne in the movies was John Riggins in real life. The guy could do everything. He was a man's man. He's one of the most colorful characters ever."

# Record Setters

When Charley Taylor retired, he didn't worry about the games he missed because of injuries, robbing him of more opportunities to catch passes. He only knew that no other receiver had come close to his numbers. "All one can ask for is to be at the top of the game when he gives it up," he said. And that's where Taylor stood: at the top. So, too, did three other Redskins when they retired.

# Charley Taylor

He dreamed of being "The Next Jim Brown," a label he'd privately given himself. Others thought differently. They'd see him zip past his blockers on a sweep, running too undisciplined to help an offense. And they gave him another label—receiver.

It's one that Charley Taylor didn't like. Another group agreed with him. They were called defensive backs, and there's no way they could have been happy when Taylor was switched from running back in 1966 to receiver. By the time he was finished in 1977, no one had caught more passes than Taylor's 649. He also grabbed 79 touchdown passes. Funny thing is, Taylor even now claims, "I never felt comfortable. I was afraid out there every weekend."

Imagine how the defenders felt. Taylor finished with 50 or more receptions in seven straight seasons. That's hardly an impressive stat in today's pass-happy offenses. But keep in mind that because of rules changes, today's receivers face much less resistance from defensive backs. Also, he never played in the era of sixteen regular season games.

One more thing: In the time Taylor played receiver (1966–77), there were only forty-four 1,000-yard seasons by players at that position. From 2001 to 2003, there were sixty-one such seasons.

And if not for injuries, Taylor could have padded his total by another 100 catches. He missed eight games in 1971, all of 1976, and half of 1977 because of various injuries. He also spent his first two seasons at running back, earning rookie of the year honors in 1964. Not that Taylor fretted over what-ifs. Besides, Taylor remained the NFL's all-time leading receiver until 1987, when Seattle's Steve Largent broke his record. In all, Taylor finished with 10,803 combined yards and 90 touchdowns.

When Taylor first switched to receiver, he had a hard time remembering assignments. That's why the first person he scared was himself. Taylor said that after coach Otto Graham told him about the move, he lost fifteen pounds from stress alone. "Sonny would call a play and I'd go, 'Yeah, that's a 15-yard in. You've got to do this, got to do that,'" Taylor said. "Actually, it would be a 15-yard out. I was like, 'God, how many mistakes can I make?' The main thing that pulled me through?—Sonny Jurgensen. He had faith in me and kept saying, 'Don't worry about it. It'll be all right.'"

Receiving wasn't his only strength. Few blocked better and harder than Taylor. Some—notably Dallas fans—also viewed his blocking with suspicion, claiming his hits to be less than fair. But Taylor scoffs at those views, saying he never made a cheap hit, always cracking back legally. In turn, Cowboys fans point to a hit he made on linebacker Chuck Howley in 1972. The crackback blew out Howley's knee, ending his season. Taylor, a native of the Dallas suburb Grand Prairie, felt the wrath. "It was a legal block," Taylor said. "For the next couple months my mom had threatening phone calls. I can't repeat what they said to her, but it wasn't pretty. I had brothers and sisters in school and they were being taunted."

His blocking earned him great respect among his teammates. But that was just one of many facets of his game. And the Howley hit was but a mere blip on his football résumé. He had great seasons—in 1966 he led the NFL with 72 receptions and 12 touchdowns while finishing with 1,119 receiving yards. He had great games—he caught 2 touchdown passes in the 1972 NFC Championship Game win over Dallas. And his final big moment came in 1975, when he entered the season finale against Philadelphia needing one catch to become the NFL's all-time leading receiver. He finally got it in the fourth quarter of a 26–3 loss at RFK Stadium, catching an 11-yard slant pass from Joe Theismann. "The stands were still full, but after the catch they emptied out," Taylor said. "We were losing the game so it wasn't a big deal. But I said, 'Damn, I'm glad this is over with.' I could breathe easier."

Defensive backs felt the same way two years later. That's when Taylor finally retired.

## Art Monk

A month or so after she joined their new company, Charles Mann's mother asked her son how he felt she was doing. She wondered because his partner rarely said anything to her. Of course, he rarely spoke to anybody. Mann reassured his mother that his partner, Art Monk, liked her and respected her; he just didn't let her know, saying to her what he had said to many over the years: very little. "Three, four months later she's laughing and joking with him," Mann said. "But Art never changed. He was who he was."

That's not the only way Monk hasn't changed since leaving the NFL. "He pays attention to detail," Mann said. "He's very meticulous, methodical, and just shows up every day. He doesn't make a lot of noise. A lot of times you forget he's in the office, then I see the results of his sales."

And that's exactly how Monk was with the Redskins. He was easy to overlook because he never drew attention to himself. He'd perform the detail work of a receiver, catching passes over the middle, blocking, and running nonglamorous routes. But the results were more than impressive.

Monk finished with 940 career receptions, 888 of which came with the Redskins. He set an NFL record with 106 receptions in 1984, the first pro receiver to surpass 100 catches in twenty years. But no catch by Monk was celebrated more than his record-breaking 820th career reception in a Monday night win over Denver at RFK Stadium. After the reception, a 10-yard down and out, teammates hoisted Monk onto their shoulders as the crowd roared its approval.

He left Washington after the 1993 season, playing one season with the New York Jets and one with Philadelphia. But his mark, clearly, was made with the Redskins, who drafted him in the first round in 1980 out of Syracuse. They landed a receiver intent on defeating his fear of failure through hard work. As a college freshman, Monk remembered dropping too many passes, calling that season a disaster. That fear throttled him, leading him to "train like crazy." He did every drill possible, training five days a week, running routes as hard as he could every time. The next

*Wide receiver Art Monk is hoisted by his teammates after breaking the record for career receptions in 1992. Wilfredo Lee/AP*

season? He caught 41 passes for 590 yards—and dropped maybe one ball.

But that was nothing compared to what happened his rookie season when neighbor and Redskins back Terry Metcalf provided him a real-life tutorial on hard work. They'd run at 9:00 A.M. every day at a high school track, doing agility work and stairs. They'd play eight games of racquetball in the afternoon and at night would play basketball, jog, or ride bikes—sometimes as many as 40 miles in a day.

After Metcalf retired following that season, Monk maintained the pace. He became infamous for his workouts at George Mason University, where he'd run 25 times uphill, doing leg-pumps; run 25 times backward; run stutter-step 25 times; run six 220-yard dashes; and run six 110-yard dashes. The first time fellow receiver Gary Clark trained with him, he told Monk, "You're crazy! I'll do my own program."

Monk would run sprints with a parachute harnessed to his back. He'd run 800s and 400s and 200s. "I'd run with him over at Mason," former Redskins running back Earnest Byner said. "It was a different level of workout for me. We'd also do extra work after practice in training camp. We'd run a mile, but we had to do it in a certain time. When we were in meetings, and he'd already been in this offense seven, eight years, he took notes like he was a rookie."

He wasn't all work. Clark once recalled Monk still shooting spitballs across the room during meetings late in his career. Another time he hid Gerald Riggs's helmet in the weeds at a practice. But work is what Monk liked best. There's a reason he pushed himself so hard. "It seemed like, no matter how well I did, I always felt like it wasn't good enough," Monk once said. So he pushed even harder, and he did it gracefully, never boasting about his accomplishments. Talking just wasn't something Monk did frequently, even to teammates. Former teammate Darrell Green recalled two-hour drives home from training camp in Carlisle, Pennsylvania, done in silence. "He didn't have a lot to say, even in meetings," Byner said.

He did once. In 1990 Monk called a team meeting with the Redskins struggling at 6–5. Many players wondered who had called the meeting, and Clark remembered thinking that some "jerk" had called it. When they found out it was Monk, Clark said, "It got our attention." Monk told the assembled group that he was going to continue fighting that season, imploring others to do the same. The Redskins went on to win four of the last five games, winning a playoff game as well. But Monk retreated back into silence. He even would turn down opportunities to make $10,000 for a speaking engagement. "People wanted more of him," longtime Redskins trainer Bubba Tyer said. "But he wasn't one of the public relation department's favorites. He had so many requests, but he denied so many things. In this era when there are so many self-promoters, if he was that way he'd be in the Hall of Fame by now. But he wasn't that way. I always called him Mr. Redskin because he was the consummate pro."

Ah, the Hall of Fame, the sticking point for Monk backers, who can't understand why he's not yet in Canton. His detractors, led by *Sports Illustrated*'s Peter King, point to his number of touchdown catches (68), low for a modern-day receiver, and Pro Bowls (three). Others say Clark was a more feared receiver. His supporters point to Monk's total catches, his approach to the game, and his willingness to sacrifice for the team.

But Monk's job was to sustain drives, and no one did that better. His routes might have been simplistic at times—many 5-yard slant patterns or out patterns. But few were more effective in doing their job. Just listen to his supporters:

Joe Theismann: "Art Monk was as great a player as a James Lofton, Lynn Swann, John Stallworth. Art didn't have the spectacular play that everyone can focus on, like Lynn Swann's catches in the Super Bowl. But you tell people Art had three times as many catches as Swann and they don't realize that.

"Art would wear a chain with a dollar sign, and I called him Big Money because he was money for us. He was my favorite receiver. I've always described Art this way: If you could spend a day with Art Monk, your life would improve by 10 percent because of the quality of the man, the work ethic, the intelligence. I've never known a better football player."

Charley Casserly: "He was Mr. Consistency on and off the field. He was the Joe DiMaggio of the Redskins. He was a quiet, classy guy who went out and did his job and made it look easy. He should be in the Hall of Fame and it's wrong that he's not. They get into how many Pro Bowls and how many dominating games did you have? My counter is that when he retired from the game he had the longest consecutive streak of catching passes of anyone in football [183] and he had the most receptions. He did it without being featured. He caught 100 balls when no one would catch 100 balls."

Joe Gibbs: "Art was unselfish. We asked him to block and run those inside routes. If we had played him on the outside, he would have had more touchdowns."

Mark Rypien: "Art is the greatest player I ever played with. It was his unbelievable commitment to himself and to us."

But Monk doesn't jump into the conversation, often saying it's not something he worries about. He's done his job; it's up to the voters to give their approval. Maybe they missed plays like this one that former special teams coach Wayne Sevier replayed to his unit in 1991. Late in a blowout win over Atlanta, Monk caught a pass on the sidelines for a first down. A Falcon defender had Monk pinned on the sideline. Rather than step out of bounds, Monk rammed the defender, gaining a few extra yards. Sevier, upset with his unit's performance late in this game, showed them the clip of Monk over and over, telling them, "Here's a guy going to the Hall of Fame and watch what he does here."

Such plays aren't bound for postgame highlights. They stick in the minds of those who watched him on a daily basis. "He didn't get the recognition he should have gotten when he was doing all those things," Casserly said. "But at the end of his career, you're like, 'Oh my god, look what this guy has done.'"

## Brian Mitchell

As a young player in high school and then in college, Brian Mitchell vowed never to return kicks, eyeing those who did so with suspicion. "I thought it was the most dangerous position ever," he said. But it turns out he was a perfect fit for that spot, and he learned that fast, returning his first NFL kickoff 92 yards for a touchdown in a 1990 preseason game against Atlanta. "The fact I had success early made me have the desire to want to be good," Mitchell said. "If I had been knocked out on that first play, I would have packed my bags and gone to Canada to play quarterback."

Mitchell played quarterback at Southwest Louisiana State and was drafted by Saskatchewan of the Canadian Football League to play quarterback. Fortunately for the Redskins, the fifth-round pick fulfilled his desire to play in the NFL, giving them the best returner in their history—and the most prolific in NFL history.

Mitchell holds nine club punt- and kick-return records. He leads in combined return yardage with 13,062—second-place Mike Nelms had 6,076. He holds the NFL record with13 return touchdowns and trails only Jerry Rice for most combined yards. Mitchell's final total of 19,013 combined return yards is 6,010 ahead of second-place Mel Gray.

Mitchell added punt returns to his duties in 1991, returning one 69 yards for a score in the season opener against Detroit. His biggest game was in 1996, when he set a club record with 240 combined return yards in a loss at Denver.

In a 1990 game at Philadelphia, both Redskins quarterbacks, starter Jeff Rutledge and backup Stan Humphries, were knocked from the game. Mitchell, a rookie, entered in the fourth quarter. He led Washington on a touchdown drive, completing 3 of 6 passes for 40 yards and scoring on a 1-yard run. "I remember telling one of my buddies that I was going to play quarterback in the NFL, even if it was just one play," said Mitchell. "To get that chance my first year on *Monday Night Football* . . . I just remember thinking that my friends and family will get a chance to see me play quarterback. I wasn't really nervous, but I was shocked when they said I was going in."

He was a little shocked at how his career unfolded, too. "I was never happy with what I did, and I always tried to be the best," Mitchell said. "But never in a million years did I think all these things would happen."

# Darrell Green

Outside the locker rooms at Dickinson College in 1994, a reporter, in his first season covering the Redskins, approached Darrell Green with a request. He just wanted a minute of his time. Green looked at his watch, his body inching toward the exit, his eyes saying he'd rather not. "Oh, man, I've got to go," Green said. But he relented, telling the reporter, "I've got two minutes."

Twenty minutes later the interview ended, revealing to the reporter a truth about Green, one consistent throughout his career: He always gave more than could be expected. That was never more true than what Green gave on the football field, where he wowed with his speed and amazed with his longevity. By the time he retired after the 2002 season, Green had played in more games than any corner in NFL history (295).

At 5'9" and 184 pounds, Green wasn't blessed with great size. But he ran a 4.2 in the 40-yard dash and that speed, and coverage ability, transformed the Redskins defense for most of his time in Washington. Former defensive coordinator Richie Petitbon used to say that Green "had as much to do with our success during the eighties and nineties as anybody."

"He was the best player during the period I was there," said Casserly, who was with Washington from 1977 to 2000. "And you'd have to put him up in the top two or three Redskins of all time. You've got Sammy Baugh and then this guy is next. He was the best player at his position for a long, long time."

He jumped into the public consciousness in his first NFL game, a 1983 Monday Night Football matchup against Dallas. NFL Films still shows the clip all the time: Dallas running back Tony Dorsett sprinting down the left sideline; Green gaining on him from the other side; Green tackling him, ending a 77-yard run short of the goal line.

As much as Green liked that play, he also knows it was harder running from it than making it. "It took me four years to show that 'This guy can cover,'" Green said. "I didn't want to just be known as a fast guy." And maybe he wouldn't have been—if tackle Darryl Grant had done his job. On that play Grant was fooled out of position, vacating the hole Dorsett ran through. "I

*Darrell Green returning an interception against the Arizona Cardinals in 1999.*
Doug Mills/AP

joke with him, 'I made you famous,'" Grant said.

Grant, of course, knows better. What made Green famous was his performance on the field, giving him a spot among the all-time greats. He earned seven trips to the Pro Bowl, the last coming in 1997 at age thirty-seven. Some years, notably 1991, Green said, "They couldn't even complete a pass on me in practice."

## Speedster

Former Redskins cornerback Darrell Green won the NFL's Fastest Man Competition three times. Green was a world-class sprinter in college at Texas A & I and once considered competing in the Olympics.

Speed wasn't the only reason he lasted twenty years and played at a high level. "This guy has to be a tough sucker to play all those years," Casserly said. "He'd come up and tackle you. He had great quickness, change of direction, and jumping ability. That's what made him a heck of a cover guy. Plus he's highly competitive and has a lot of pride. He never backed down from a challenge."

"He just knew how to get it done," Mann said. "He didn't have the most conventional style of covering. His former coaches would all say to a man that he had the worst technique of any cornerback. But it was his gamesmanship and desire to succeed. Some people make excuses all the time for lack of whatever, and he never did that." That competitive desire is why he'd always get a little more excited facing receivers such as Roy Green or Mike Quick or Jerry Rice or Michael Irvin. All of them not only were great, but they matched Darrell Green's competitiveness.

Green remained a full-time starter until his final three seasons, agreeing to be a backup when the Redskins signed Deion Sanders to pair with Champ Bailey in 2000. But during those seventeen years, few Redskins provided more highlights.

There was a 72-yard interception return for a touchdown against the Rams in the 1983 playoffs; 3 interceptions against Detroit in 1987; and interception returns for touchdowns against Detroit in the NFC Championship Game after the 1991 season followed two weeks later by the same feat in the Super Bowl win over Buffalo. The 52-yard punt return for a score against Chicago in a 1987 playoff win is among the most remembered plays in Redskins history. No one who watched that play can forget: Green clutching his side as he leapt over Cap Boso en route to the end zone. Green had torn rib cartilage on the play.

He nearly didn't play the following week in the NFC Championship Game against Minnesota. But after much soul-searching and prayer, Green took a pain-killing shot enabling him to play. On fourth and goal from the Redskins' 6 in the final minute of a 17–10 game, Minnesota quarterback Wade Wilson threw to running back Darrin Nelson at the 1 yard line. Green, reading the play perfectly, arrived the same time as the ball, jarring it free. Or so it appeared. "I looked like I was a hero," Green said. "Everyone thought I knocked it out, but Nelson wouldn't have caught the ball anyway."

And in his last game, he sped 35 yards on a punt-return reverse, leaping over a Cowboy to give fans one last thrill and reminding them of the Bears play.

But his play isn't the only reason he was so beloved. Green became—and has remained—a vital part of the community, starting his Youth Life Foundation. He's also started Darrell Green Enterprises. The foundation and his community work are the reasons why the Virginia General Assembly named the Loudoun County portion of Route 28 Darrell Green Boulevard.

"And that was a unanimous decision," Green said. "I'm always amazed at these things, the favor God has put on my life. If I'm ever not amazed, then something is wrong with me."

The deeply religious Green is proudest of not just playing for twenty years, but staying in one city, where he could raise his son and daughter with his wife. Family means more to Green than anything. "If I went after the money, I would have played for eight teams, minimum," Green said. "I wouldn't trade this for a zillion dollars. The normal person says, 'You still made a million dollars.' That's pretty good but I would have made tens of millions. My biggest bonus was around a million. In my heyday?—goodness! But I'm not complaining or patting myself on the back. But I did become who I wanted to become without really trying to. I was just doing it."

He's still doing it, with ten learning centers and counting. And his former teammates haven't stopped marveling at him. "He was the ultimate professional," former teammate and corner Barry Wilburn said. "I remember back then [in the 1980s] he knew he would play twenty years. He would talk about it and say, 'If I don't get hurt and keep my legs in shape then I can.' I believed it. He was just special."

# About the Author

**John Keim** has covered the Washington Redskins since 1994, first as a beat reporter for The Journal Newspapers and now as a columnist for the *Washington Examiner*. He's also the editor of *Warpath* magazine and warpathinsiders.com. He has authored several books, including *Hail to RFK: 36 Seasons of Redskins Memories*; *America's Rivalry: The 20 Greatest Redskins-Cowboys Games*; and *Legends by the Lake: The Cleveland Browns at Municipal Stadium*. He lives in Centreville, Virginia, with his wife, Kerry, and sons Matthew, Christopher, and Sean.